50 Zero-Waste Cooking Recipes for Home

By: Kelly Johnson

Table of Contents

- Vegetable Scrap Broth
- Banana Peel Cake
- Carrot Top Pesto
- Citrus Peel Cleaner
- Stale Bread Croutons
- Pickled Watermelon Rind
- Potato Peel Chips
- Beet Green Chips
- Kale Stem Pesto
- Apple Core Jelly
- Pumpkin Seed Pesto
- Cauliflower Leaf Stir Fry
- Radish Top Soup
- Broccoli Stem Slaw
- Avocado Seed Smoothie
- Citrus Peel Candy
- Herb Stem Salt
- Berry Pulp Muffins
- Tomato Skin Powder
- Celery Leaf Salad
- Orange Peel Vinegar
- Pineapple Core Jam
- Coffee Ground Body Scrub
- Leftover Vegetable Stir Fry
- Corn Husk Tamales
- Watermelon Seed Butter
- Apple Peel Tea
- Onion Skin Dye
- Bell Pepper Seed Hummus
- Lemon Rind Sorbet
- Carrot Top Chimichurri
- Broccoli Stem Soup
- Cucumber Peel Salad
- Sweet Potato Skin Chips
- Citrus Peel Infused Oil

- Herb Stem Infused Vinegar
- Banana Peel Vegan Bacon
- Leftover Rice Fritters
- Veggie Scrap Quiche
- Stale Bread Pudding
- Kale Stem Chips
- Beet Stem Stir Fry
- Potato Peel Soup
- Avocado Seed Guacamole
- Tomato Skin Salsa
- Radish Top Pesto
- Citrus Peel Marmalade
- Apple Core Vinegar
- Pineapple Core Smoothie
- Coffee Grounds Marinade

Vegetable Scrap Broth

Ingredients:

- Vegetable scraps (such as carrot peels, onion skins, celery tops, mushroom stems, garlic cloves, etc.)
- Water
- Optional: herbs like parsley, thyme, bay leaves
- Optional: salt and pepper to taste

Instructions:

Collect Vegetable Scraps: Save vegetable scraps from your cooking endeavors. This could include things like carrot peels, onion ends, celery leaves, mushroom stems, and any other vegetable trimmings you have on hand. Store these scraps in a resealable bag or container in the freezer until you have enough to make broth.

Prepare the Broth: Once you've accumulated a good amount of vegetable scraps, place them in a large pot. You can use a variety of scraps for a more complex flavor. Add any optional herbs you'd like to include.

Cover with Water: Pour enough water into the pot to cover the vegetable scraps by an inch or two.

Simmer: Bring the pot to a boil over high heat, then reduce the heat to low and let the broth simmer gently for about 30 minutes to an hour. This allows the flavors to meld and develop.

Strain: Once the broth has simmered and developed flavor, remove it from the heat and let it cool slightly. Then, strain the broth through a fine-mesh sieve or cheesecloth into another pot or large bowl to remove the vegetable solids. Press down on the solids to extract as much liquid as possible.

Season (optional): Taste the broth and season with salt and pepper as desired. Keep in mind that the broth will be used as a base for other dishes, so you may not need much additional seasoning.

Storage: Once cooled, you can use the broth immediately in your favorite recipes, or store it in airtight containers in the refrigerator for up to a week, or freeze it for longer storage. Be sure to label the containers with the date.

Usage: Use your homemade vegetable scrap broth as a base for soups, stews, sauces, and risottos, or any recipe that calls for broth or stock.

This method not only produces a flavorful broth but also reduces food waste by utilizing parts of vegetables that are often discarded. It's an economical and sustainable way to add depth and richness to your cooking.

Banana Peel Cake

Ingredients:

- 2 ripe bananas
- 2 cups all-purpose flour
- 1 cup sugar
- 1/2 cup vegetable oil or melted butter
- 2 eggs
- 1 teaspoon vanilla extract
- 1 teaspoon baking powder
- 1/2 teaspoon baking soda
- 1/2 teaspoon salt
- 1/2 teaspoon ground cinnamon (optional)
- 1/4 cup milk (optional, if needed for consistency)

Instructions:

Prepare the Banana Peels: Wash the banana peels thoroughly to remove any dirt or residue. Trim off the ends and discard them. Chop the banana peels into small pieces and then blend them in a food processor or blender until smooth. If necessary, add a small amount of water to help with blending.

Preheat the Oven: Preheat your oven to 350°F (175°C). Grease and flour a 9x13-inch baking pan or line it with parchment paper.

Mix Wet Ingredients: In a large mixing bowl, mash the ripe bananas with a fork until smooth. Add the blended banana peels, sugar, vegetable oil or melted butter, eggs, and vanilla extract. Mix until well combined.

Combine Dry Ingredients: In a separate bowl, whisk together the all-purpose flour, baking powder, baking soda, salt, and ground cinnamon (if using).

Combine Wet and Dry Ingredients: Gradually add the dry ingredients to the wet ingredients, stirring until just combined. Be careful not to overmix, as this can result in a dense cake.

Adjust Consistency: If the batter seems too thick, you can add a little milk, one tablespoon at a time, until you reach the desired consistency. The batter should be thick but pourable.

Bake the Cake: Pour the batter into the prepared baking pan and spread it evenly. Bake in the preheated oven for 25-30 minutes, or until a toothpick inserted into the center comes out clean.

Cool and Serve: Allow the cake to cool in the pan for about 10 minutes, then transfer it to a wire rack to cool completely. Once cooled, slice the cake and serve it plain or with your favorite frosting or glaze.

This banana peel cake is moist, flavorful, and a great way to reduce food waste by using parts of the banana that are often discarded. It's a delicious treat that's sure to surprise and impress your friends and family!

Carrot Top Pesto

Ingredients:

- 2 cups carrot tops, washed and dried
- 1/2 cup fresh basil leaves (optional, for added flavor)
- 1/3 cup nuts (such as pine nuts, walnuts, or almonds), toasted
- 2 cloves garlic, peeled
- 1/2 cup grated Parmesan cheese (or nutritional yeast for a vegan option)
- 1/2 cup extra-virgin olive oil
- Salt and pepper to taste
- Optional: lemon juice or zest for brightness

Instructions:

Prepare Carrot Tops: Wash the carrot tops thoroughly under cold water to remove any dirt or debris. Trim off any tough stems, leaving just the tender leaves.
Toast Nuts: In a dry skillet over medium heat, toast the nuts until fragrant and lightly browned, stirring occasionally to prevent burning. Remove from heat and let cool.
Blend Ingredients: In a food processor or blender, combine the carrot tops, basil leaves (if using), toasted nuts, garlic cloves, and grated Parmesan cheese. Pulse several times until the ingredients are coarsely chopped and combined.
Add Olive Oil: With the food processor or blender running, slowly drizzle in the olive oil until the mixture comes together into a thick paste. You may need to stop and scrape down the sides of the bowl with a spatula to ensure all ingredients are incorporated.
Season: Taste the pesto and season with salt and pepper to your liking. If desired, add a squeeze of lemon juice or a pinch of lemon zest for brightness.
Adjust Consistency: If the pesto is too thick, you can thin it out with additional olive oil, a tablespoon at a time, until you reach the desired consistency.
Serve or Store: Transfer the carrot top pesto to a jar or airtight container. It can be used immediately as a spread, dip, or sauce, or stored in the refrigerator for up to a week. You can also freeze it in ice cube trays for longer storage.

Carrot top pesto is a versatile condiment that can be used in various dishes, such as pasta, sandwiches, salads, roasted vegetables, and more. It's a flavorful way to reduce food waste and add a unique twist to your meals!

Citrus Peel Cleaner

Ingredients:

- Citrus peels (lemons, oranges, or any citrus fruit)
- White vinegar
- Water

Instructions:

Collect Citrus Peels: Gather citrus peels from lemons, oranges, or any other citrus fruits you have on hand. Make sure to remove any fruit pulp as much as possible, as it can cause the cleaner to become cloudy.

Prepare a Jar: Find a clean, empty glass jar with a tight-fitting lid.

Fill the Jar with Peels: Place the citrus peels into the jar until it's about halfway full.

Add White Vinegar: Pour white vinegar into the jar, covering the citrus peels completely. Leave some space at the top of the jar to allow for expansion.

Let it Infuse: Seal the jar tightly and let it sit in a cool, dark place for about 1 to 2 weeks. During this time, the vinegar will absorb the citrus oils and become infused with their scent and cleaning properties.

Strain the Cleaner: After the infusion period, strain the citrus-infused vinegar into a clean spray bottle or container, discarding the citrus peels.

Dilute (Optional): If the vinegar scent is too strong for your liking, you can dilute the citrus-infused vinegar with water. A common ratio is 1 part citrus-infused vinegar to 1 part water, but you can adjust this to suit your preference.

Usage: Use the citrus peel cleaner as you would any other all-purpose cleaner. It's effective for cleaning surfaces like countertops, sinks, and appliances. It also works well for removing soap scum and hard water stains in the bathroom.

Storage: Store the citrus peel cleaner in a cool, dark place when not in use. It should last for several weeks to a few months, depending on the storage conditions.

This homemade citrus peel cleaner is natural, non-toxic, and environmentally friendly. It's a great alternative to commercial cleaners that may contain harsh chemicals, and it leaves your home smelling fresh and citrusy!

Stale Bread Croutons

Ingredients:

- Stale bread (any type, such as French bread, baguette, ciabatta, etc.)
- Olive oil or melted butter
- Salt
- Optional seasonings (such as garlic powder, onion powder, dried herbs like thyme or rosemary, grated Parmesan cheese, etc.)

Instructions:

Preheat the Oven: Preheat your oven to 375°F (190°C).

Prepare the Bread: Slice or tear the stale bread into bite-sized pieces. You can remove the crusts if you prefer, but they can also be left on for added texture.

Season the Bread: In a bowl, toss the bread pieces with olive oil or melted butter until they're evenly coated. Sprinkle with salt and any additional seasonings you'd like to use. Mix well to ensure the seasonings are evenly distributed.

Bake the Croutons: Spread the seasoned bread pieces in a single layer on a baking sheet. Make sure they're not overcrowded to allow for even baking.

Bake in the Preheated Oven: Place the baking sheet in the preheated oven and bake for about 10-15 minutes, or until the croutons are golden brown and crisp, stirring halfway through to ensure even baking.

Cool and Store: Once the croutons are done baking, remove them from the oven and let them cool completely on the baking sheet. They will continue to crisp up as they cool.

Serve or Store: Use the croutons immediately in your favorite salads, soups, or other dishes. Alternatively, let them cool completely before transferring them to an airtight container for storage. Stale bread croutons will keep for several days at room temperature.

Stale bread croutons are a simple and delicious way to breathe new life into old bread. Experiment with different seasonings and types of bread to create croutons that complement your favorite dishes perfectly!

Pickled Watermelon Rind

Ingredients:

- Stale bread (any type, such as French bread, baguette, ciabatta, etc.)
- Olive oil or melted butter
- Salt
- Optional seasonings (such as garlic powder, onion powder, dried herbs like thyme or rosemary, grated Parmesan cheese, etc.)

Instructions:

Preheat the Oven: Preheat your oven to 375°F (190°C).
Prepare the Bread: Slice or tear the stale bread into bite-sized pieces. You can remove the crusts if you prefer, but they can also be left on for added texture.
Season the Bread: In a bowl, toss the bread pieces with olive oil or melted butter until they're evenly coated. Sprinkle with salt and any additional seasonings you'd like to use. Mix well to ensure the seasonings are evenly distributed.
Bake the Croutons: Spread the seasoned bread pieces in a single layer on a baking sheet. Make sure they're not overcrowded to allow for even baking.
Bake in the Preheated Oven: Place the baking sheet in the preheated oven and bake for about 10-15 minutes, or until the croutons are golden brown and crisp, stirring halfway through to ensure even baking.
Cool and Store: Once the croutons are done baking, remove them from the oven and let them cool completely on the baking sheet. They will continue to crisp up as they cool.
Serve or Store: Use the croutons immediately in your favorite salads, soups, or other dishes. Alternatively, let them cool completely before transferring them to an airtight container for storage. Stale bread croutons will keep for several days at room temperature.

Stale bread croutons are a simple and delicious way to breathe new life into old bread. Experiment with different seasonings and types of bread to create croutons that complement your favorite dishes perfectly!

Potato Peel Chips

Ingredients:

- Potato peels (from 2-3 potatoes)
- Olive oil or vegetable oil
- Salt
- Optional seasonings (such as garlic powder, paprika, cayenne pepper, dried herbs, grated Parmesan cheese, etc.)

Instructions:

Prepare Potato Peels: Wash the potatoes thoroughly under cold water to remove any dirt or debris. Using a vegetable peeler or knife, peel the potatoes, making sure to leave a thin layer of flesh on the peels. Save the peeled potatoes for another use.

Dry Potato Peels: Pat the potato peels dry with a clean kitchen towel or paper towels to remove excess moisture. The drier the peels, the crispier the chips will be.

Season the Peels: In a bowl, toss the dry potato peels with a drizzle of olive oil or vegetable oil until they're evenly coated. Sprinkle with salt and any additional seasonings you'd like to use. Mix well to ensure the seasonings are evenly distributed.

Bake the Chips: Preheat your oven to 375°F (190°C). Spread the seasoned potato peels in a single layer on a baking sheet lined with parchment paper or a silicone baking mat. Make sure they're not overlapping to allow for even baking.

Bake in the Preheated Oven: Place the baking sheet in the preheated oven and bake for about 15-20 minutes, or until the potato peels are golden brown and crispy, stirring halfway through to ensure even cooking.

Cool and Serve: Once the potato peel chips are done baking, remove them from the oven and let them cool slightly on the baking sheet. They will continue to crisp up as they cool. Serve the chips warm as a snack or side dish.

Potato peel chips are a tasty and sustainable way to reduce food waste while enjoying a crunchy snack. Experiment with different seasonings to customize the flavor to your liking. Enjoy!

Beet Green Chips

Ingredients:

- Beet greens (from 2-3 beets)
- Olive oil or vegetable oil
- Salt
- Optional seasonings (such as garlic powder, onion powder, paprika, cayenne pepper, grated Parmesan cheese, etc.)

Instructions:

Prepare Beet Greens: Wash the beet greens thoroughly under cold water to remove any dirt or debris. Trim off any tough stems, leaving just the tender leaves. Pat them dry with a clean kitchen towel or paper towels to remove excess moisture.

Preheat the Oven: Preheat your oven to 325°F (160°C).

Season the Greens: In a bowl, toss the dry beet greens with a drizzle of olive oil or vegetable oil until they're evenly coated. Sprinkle with salt and any additional seasonings you'd like to use. Mix well to ensure the seasonings are evenly distributed.

Bake the Chips: Line a baking sheet with parchment paper or a silicone baking mat. Spread the seasoned beet greens in a single layer on the baking sheet, making sure they're not overlapping.

Bake in the Preheated Oven: Place the baking sheet in the preheated oven and bake for about 10-15 minutes, or until the beet greens are crispy and starting to turn golden brown, checking them frequently to prevent burning.

Cool and Serve: Once the beet green chips are done baking, remove them from the oven and let them cool slightly on the baking sheet. They will continue to crisp up as they cool. Serve the chips warm as a snack or side dish.

Beet green chips are a nutritious alternative to potato chips and a great way to reduce food waste by using the entire beet. Experiment with different seasonings to customize the flavor to your liking. Enjoy!

Kale Stem Pesto

Ingredients:

- Kale stems (from a bunch of kale), chopped into smaller pieces
- 2 cloves garlic, peeled
- 1/4 cup nuts (such as pine nuts, walnuts, or almonds), toasted
- 1/2 cup grated Parmesan cheese (or nutritional yeast for a vegan option)
- 1/2 cup extra-virgin olive oil
- Salt and pepper to taste

Instructions:

Prepare Kale Stems: Wash the kale stems thoroughly under cold water to remove any dirt or debris. Trim off any tough or fibrous ends, leaving just the tender parts of the stems. Chop the stems into smaller pieces.

Boil or Steam Kale Stems: Bring a pot of water to a boil and add the chopped kale stems. Boil for about 5-7 minutes, or until the stems are tender. Alternatively, you can steam the kale stems until they are soft. Drain the cooked kale stems and let them cool slightly.

Toast Nuts: In a dry skillet over medium heat, toast the nuts until fragrant and lightly browned, stirring occasionally to prevent burning. Remove from heat and let cool.

Blend Ingredients: In a food processor or blender, combine the cooked kale stems, peeled garlic cloves, toasted nuts, and grated Parmesan cheese. Pulse several times until the ingredients are finely chopped and well combined.

Add Olive Oil: With the food processor or blender running, slowly drizzle in the olive oil until the mixture comes together into a thick paste. You may need to stop and scrape down the sides of the bowl with a spatula to ensure all ingredients are incorporated.

Season: Taste the pesto and season with salt and pepper to your liking. Adjust the consistency by adding more olive oil if needed.

Serve or Store: Transfer the kale stem pesto to a jar or airtight container. It can be used immediately as a spread, dip, or sauce, or stored in the refrigerator for up to a week. You can also freeze it in ice cube trays for longer storage.

Kale stem pesto is a nutritious and flavorful condiment that can be used in pasta dishes, sandwiches, wraps, and more. It's a great way to reduce food waste and add a unique twist to your meals!

Apple Core Jelly

Ingredients:

- Apple cores and peels (from about 8-10 medium-sized apples)
- Water
- Sugar
- Lemon juice

Instructions:

Prepare Apple Cores and Peels: Collect the cores and peels from about 8-10 medium-sized apples. Make sure to remove any seeds or stems from the cores.

Simmer the Cores and Peels: Place the apple cores and peels in a large pot and cover them with water. Bring the water to a boil, then reduce the heat to low and let the mixture simmer for about 30-45 minutes. This will extract the flavor and natural pectin from the apple cores and peels.

Strain the Liquid: After simmering, strain the liquid through a fine-mesh sieve or cheesecloth into another pot or large bowl to separate the apple solids from the liquid. Press down on the solids to extract as much liquid as possible.

Measure the Liquid: Measure the strained liquid and return it to the pot. For every cup of liquid, add 1 cup of sugar and 1 tablespoon of lemon juice. Stir well to dissolve the sugar.

Cook the Jelly: Bring the mixture to a boil over medium-high heat, then reduce the heat to low and let it simmer gently. Skim off any foam that rises to the surface.

Test for Doneness: To test if the jelly is done, you can use a candy thermometer to check the temperature. Jelly is typically ready when it reaches 220°F (104°C). You can also perform a "wrinkle test" by placing a small amount of jelly on a chilled plate. If it wrinkles when you push your finger through it, it's ready.

Prepare Jars: While the jelly is cooking, prepare sterilized jars for canning. You can do this by washing the jars and lids in hot, soapy water, then placing them in a pot of boiling water for a few minutes to sterilize.

Fill Jars and Seal: Once the jelly is done, carefully ladle it into the prepared jars, leaving a quarter-inch of headspace at the top. Wipe the rims of the jars clean, then seal them with the lids and bands.

Process Jars (Optional): If you'd like to store the jelly at room temperature, you can process the jars in a boiling water bath for about 10 minutes to ensure they are properly sealed. Otherwise, you can store the jelly in the refrigerator for immediate use.

Cool and Store: Let the jars of jelly cool completely before storing them in a cool, dark place. Properly sealed jars can be stored at room temperature for up to a year. Once opened, store the jelly in the refrigerator.

Apple core jelly is delicious spread on toast, biscuits, or scones, and it also makes a lovely gift when packaged in decorative jars. Enjoy your homemade jelly and the satisfaction of reducing food waste!

Pumpkin Seed Pesto

Ingredients:

- 1 cup pumpkin seeds (also known as pepitas), toasted
- 2 cloves garlic, peeled
- 1 cup fresh basil leaves
- 1/2 cup grated Parmesan cheese (or nutritional yeast for a vegan option)
- 1/2 cup extra-virgin olive oil
- Juice of 1/2 lemon
- Salt and pepper to taste

Instructions:

Toast Pumpkin Seeds: In a dry skillet over medium heat, toast the pumpkin seeds until they are lightly browned and fragrant, stirring frequently to prevent burning. This should take about 5-7 minutes. Remove from heat and let cool.

Prepare Ingredients: Peel the garlic cloves and wash the basil leaves.

Blend Ingredients: In a food processor or blender, combine the toasted pumpkin seeds, peeled garlic cloves, basil leaves, grated Parmesan cheese, and lemon juice. Pulse several times to chop the ingredients.

Add Olive Oil: With the food processor or blender running, slowly drizzle in the olive oil until the mixture comes together into a thick paste. You may need to stop and scrape down the sides of the bowl with a spatula to ensure all ingredients are incorporated.

Season: Taste the pesto and season with salt and pepper to your liking. Adjust the consistency by adding more olive oil if needed.

Serve or Store: Transfer the pumpkin seed pesto to a jar or airtight container. It can be used immediately as a spread, dip, or sauce, or stored in the refrigerator for up to a week. You can also freeze it in ice cube trays for longer storage.

Pumpkin seed pesto is versatile and delicious. Use it as a pasta sauce, spread it on sandwiches, drizzle it over roasted vegetables, or mix it into salads for added flavor.

Enjoy experimenting with this tasty alternative to traditional pesto!

Cauliflower Leaf Stir Fry

Ingredients:

- Cauliflower leaves (from 1 head of cauliflower), washed and chopped
- 2 tablespoons oil (vegetable oil, olive oil, or any cooking oil of your choice)
- 2 cloves garlic, minced
- 1 teaspoon grated ginger
- 1 small onion, thinly sliced
- 1 bell pepper, thinly sliced
- 1 carrot, julienned
- 1 cup sliced mushrooms (optional)
- Soy sauce or tamari, to taste
- Salt and pepper, to taste
- Red pepper flakes (optional, for heat)
- Sesame seeds, for garnish (optional)
- Cooked rice or noodles, for serving

Instructions:

Prepare Cauliflower Leaves: Wash the cauliflower leaves thoroughly under cold water to remove any dirt or debris. Chop the leaves into bite-sized pieces, discarding any tough stems.

Heat Oil: Heat the oil in a large skillet or wok over medium-high heat.

Sauté Aromatics: Add the minced garlic and grated ginger to the hot oil and sauté for about 30 seconds, or until fragrant.

Add Vegetables: Add the thinly sliced onion, bell pepper, carrot, and sliced mushrooms (if using) to the skillet. Stir-fry the vegetables for 3-4 minutes, or until they start to soften.

Add Cauliflower Leaves: Add the chopped cauliflower leaves to the skillet. Stir-fry everything together for another 3-4 minutes, or until the cauliflower leaves are wilted and tender.

Season: Season the stir-fry with soy sauce or tamari, salt, pepper, and red pepper flakes (if using). Adjust the seasoning to taste.

Finish and Serve: Once the vegetables are cooked to your liking, remove the skillet from the heat. Sprinkle the stir-fry with sesame seeds for garnish, if desired. Serve the cauliflower leaf stir-fry hot over cooked rice or noodles.

Cauliflower leaf stir-fry is a versatile dish that can be customized with your favorite vegetables and seasonings. It's a nutritious and flavorful way to enjoy cauliflower leaves and add variety to your meals. Enjoy!

Radish Top Soup

Ingredients:

- Radish greens (from a bunch of radishes), washed and chopped
- 1 tablespoon olive oil or butter
- 1 onion, chopped
- 2 cloves garlic, minced
- 4 cups vegetable or chicken broth
- 2 potatoes, peeled and diced
- Salt and pepper, to taste
- Optional toppings: yogurt or sour cream, chopped fresh herbs, croutons

Instructions:

Sauté Aromatics: Heat the olive oil or butter in a large pot over medium heat. Add the chopped onion and minced garlic, and sauté until the onion is translucent and fragrant, about 5 minutes.
Add Radish Greens: Add the chopped radish greens to the pot and sauté for an additional 2-3 minutes, until they begin to wilt.
Add Broth and Potatoes: Pour in the vegetable or chicken broth, and add the diced potatoes to the pot. Bring the mixture to a simmer.
Simmer: Reduce the heat to low and let the soup simmer for about 15-20 minutes, or until the potatoes are tender and cooked through.
Blend: Using an immersion blender or transferring the soup to a blender in batches, blend the soup until smooth and creamy. Be careful when blending hot liquids.
Season: Taste the soup and season with salt and pepper to your liking. Adjust the seasoning as needed.
Serve: Ladle the radish top soup into bowls and garnish with a dollop of yogurt or sour cream, chopped fresh herbs, and/or croutons, if desired. Serve hot.

Radish top soup is a delicious and nutritious way to use up radish greens and enjoy a comforting bowl of soup. It's rich in flavor and packed with vitamins and minerals.

Enjoy!

Broccoli Stem Slaw

Ingredients:

- 2 broccoli stems, peeled
- 1 carrot, peeled
- 1/4 small red cabbage, thinly sliced
- 1/4 cup mayonnaise (or Greek yogurt for a lighter option)
- 1 tablespoon apple cider vinegar
- 1 tablespoon honey or maple syrup
- 1 teaspoon Dijon mustard
- Salt and pepper, to taste
- Optional toppings: toasted nuts or seeds, dried cranberries or raisins, chopped fresh herbs

Instructions:

Prepare Vegetables: Trim off the tough ends of the broccoli stems. Using a sharp knife or vegetable peeler, peel the tough outer layer of the broccoli stems. Then, thinly slice or julienne the peeled broccoli stems and carrot. Thinly slice the red cabbage.
Make Dressing: In a small bowl, whisk together the mayonnaise (or Greek yogurt), apple cider vinegar, honey or maple syrup, Dijon mustard, salt, and pepper until smooth and well combined.
Combine Ingredients: In a large mixing bowl, combine the sliced broccoli stems, carrot, and red cabbage. Pour the dressing over the vegetables and toss until evenly coated.
Chill: Cover the bowl and refrigerate the broccoli stem slaw for at least 30 minutes to allow the flavors to meld and the vegetables to slightly soften.
Serve: Once chilled, give the slaw a final toss and transfer it to a serving bowl. Garnish with toasted nuts or seeds, dried cranberries or raisins, and chopped fresh herbs, if desired. Serve cold.

Broccoli stem slaw is a delicious and nutritious side dish or topping for sandwiches and burgers. It's a great way to use up broccoli stems and add crunch to your meals. Enjoy!

Avocado Seed Smoothie

Ingredients:

- Flesh of 1 ripe avocado
- 1 banana, fresh or frozen
- 1 cup spinach or kale leaves
- 1 cup almond milk or any milk of your choice
- 1 tablespoon honey or maple syrup (optional, for sweetness)
- 1 tablespoon avocado seed powder (prepared by drying and grinding the avocado seed)

Instructions:

Prepare Avocado Seed Powder: To make avocado seed powder, thoroughly wash and dry the avocado seed. Cut it into smaller pieces and place them in a food dehydrator or spread them on a baking sheet and dry them in the oven at a low temperature (around 200°F or 95°C) for several hours until completely dry. Once dried, grind the avocado seed pieces into a fine powder using a spice grinder or blender.

Assemble Smoothie Ingredients: In a blender, combine the flesh of the ripe avocado, banana, spinach or kale leaves, almond milk, honey or maple syrup (if using), and avocado seed powder.

Blend Until Smooth: Blend all the ingredients together until smooth and creamy. If the smoothie is too thick, you can add more almond milk to reach your desired consistency.

Taste and Adjust: Taste the smoothie and adjust the sweetness or thickness as needed by adding more honey, maple syrup, or almond milk.

Serve: Pour the avocado seed smoothie into glasses and serve immediately. You can garnish with additional slices of avocado or a sprinkle of avocado seed powder if desired.

Remember that while avocado seeds may offer potential health benefits, it's essential to consume them in moderation and consult with a healthcare professional if you have any concerns. Additionally, if you're unsure about using avocado seeds in your smoothies, you can stick to using the flesh of the avocado, which is rich in healthy fats and nutrients.

Citrus Peel Candy

Ingredients:

- Citrus fruit (such as oranges, lemons, or grapefruits)
- Water
- Sugar
- Optional: dark chocolate for dipping

Instructions:

Prepare Citrus Peels: Wash the citrus fruit thoroughly under cold water to remove any dirt or residue. Using a sharp knife or vegetable peeler, carefully peel the citrus fruit, making sure to remove as much of the outer colored zest as possible, while avoiding the bitter white pith underneath. Cut the peels into thin strips or small pieces.

Boil the Peels: Place the citrus peels in a saucepan and cover them with cold water. Bring the water to a boil, then reduce the heat and let the peels simmer for about 10 minutes. This helps to soften the peels and remove any bitterness.

Repeat Boiling Process (Optional): Drain the peels and repeat the boiling process one or two more times, using fresh water each time. This further helps to reduce bitterness.

Make Sugar Syrup: In a separate saucepan, combine equal parts water and sugar (for example, 1 cup of water and 1 cup of sugar). Heat the mixture over medium heat, stirring occasionally, until the sugar is completely dissolved and the syrup begins to simmer.

Add Citrus Peels to Syrup: Add the drained citrus peels to the sugar syrup and stir to coat them evenly. Let the peels simmer gently in the syrup for about 45 minutes to 1 hour, or until they become translucent and soft.

Drain and Cool: Using a slotted spoon, remove the citrus peels from the syrup and place them on a wire rack or parchment-lined baking sheet to cool and dry. Let them sit at room temperature for several hours or overnight until they are completely dry and slightly tacky to the touch.

Optional: Dip in Chocolate: Once the citrus peels are dry, you can dip them in melted dark chocolate for an extra indulgent treat. Simply melt the chocolate in a double boiler or microwave, dip the cooled citrus peels into the chocolate, and place them back on the wire rack or parchment paper to set.

Store: Once the chocolate (if using) has set, store the citrus peel candy in an airtight container at room temperature. They should keep for several weeks.

Enjoy your homemade citrus peel candy as a sweet snack or gift them to friends and family!

Herb Stem Salt

Ingredients:

- Herb stems (from any fresh herbs like parsley, cilantro, rosemary, thyme, etc.)
- Coarse sea salt or kosher salt

Instructions:

Collect Herb Stems: Gather herb stems from any fresh herbs you have on hand. This is a great way to use up stems that would otherwise be discarded.

Dry Herb Stems: Lay the herb stems out in a single layer on a clean kitchen towel or paper towel. Let them air dry for a few hours or overnight until they are completely dry. This step is important to prevent mold or spoilage when combined with salt.

Remove Leaves (Optional): If desired, you can strip the leaves from the herb stems and reserve them for another use, such as cooking or garnishing. However, leaving some leaves on the stems can add extra flavor to the salt.

Combine with Salt: Once the herb stems are dry, place them in a food processor or blender along with the coarse sea salt or kosher salt. The ratio of herb stems to salt can vary depending on your preference, but a common ratio is about 1 part herb stems to 4 parts salt.

Pulse or Blend: Pulse or blend the herb stems and salt together until the mixture is finely chopped and well combined. Be careful not to over-process, as you want to maintain some texture in the salt.

Spread and Dry: Spread the herb stem salt mixture out in a thin layer on a baking sheet lined with parchment paper. Let it air dry for another day or two to ensure that any remaining moisture evaporates and the flavors meld together.

Store: Once completely dry, transfer the herb stem salt to an airtight container or jar for storage. Store it in a cool, dry place away from direct sunlight. It should keep for several months.

Usage:

- Use herb stem salt as you would any other seasoning salt. Sprinkle it over roasted vegetables, grilled meats, salads, soups, or any dish where you want to add a pop of flavor.
- It also makes a thoughtful homemade gift for fellow food enthusiasts!

Enjoy experimenting with different combinations of herb stems to create your own unique herb stem salt blend.

Berry Pulp Muffins

Ingredients:

- 1 1/2 cups all-purpose flour
- 1/2 cup sugar (granulated or brown sugar)
- 1 teaspoon baking powder
- 1/2 teaspoon baking soda
- 1/4 teaspoon salt
- 1 cup berry pulp (from juicing or blending berries)
- 1/3 cup vegetable oil or melted butter
- 2 eggs
- 1 teaspoon vanilla extract
- Optional add-ins: chopped nuts, chocolate chips, or additional berries for extra flavor and texture

Instructions:

Preheat Oven: Preheat your oven to 350°F (175°C). Line a muffin tin with paper liners or grease the muffin cups.

Mix Dry Ingredients: In a large mixing bowl, whisk together the flour, sugar, baking powder, baking soda, and salt until well combined.

Combine Wet Ingredients: In a separate bowl, combine the berry pulp, vegetable oil or melted butter, eggs, and vanilla extract. Mix until smooth and well combined.

Combine Wet and Dry Ingredients: Pour the wet ingredients into the bowl of dry ingredients. Use a spatula or wooden spoon to gently fold the ingredients together until just combined. Be careful not to overmix, as this can result in tough muffins.

Add Optional Add-Ins: If using any additional add-ins such as chopped nuts, chocolate chips, or extra berries, fold them into the muffin batter gently.

Fill Muffin Cups: Spoon the batter into the prepared muffin cups, filling each cup about 2/3 full.

Bake: Place the muffin tin in the preheated oven and bake for 18-20 minutes, or until the muffins are golden brown on top and a toothpick inserted into the center comes out clean.

Cool and Serve: Remove the muffin tin from the oven and let the muffins cool in the tin for a few minutes before transferring them to a wire rack to cool completely. Serve the berry pulp muffins warm or at room temperature.

These berry pulp muffins are perfect for breakfast, brunch, or as a snack on the go. They're a delightful way to enjoy the natural sweetness and flavor of fresh berries while reducing food waste. Enjoy!

Tomato Skin Powder

Ingredients:

- Tomato skins (from fresh tomatoes)

Instructions:

Collect Tomato Skins: Gather tomato skins from fresh tomatoes. You can use the skins leftover from peeling tomatoes for sauces, soups, or other recipes.
Dry the Tomato Skins: Lay the tomato skins out in a single layer on a baking sheet lined with parchment paper or a silicone baking mat. Make sure the skins are spread out evenly and not overlapping.
Dehydrate the Skins: Place the baking sheet in an oven preheated to the lowest setting (usually around 170°F or 75°C). Alternatively, you can use a food dehydrator set to a low temperature (around 135°F or 57°C). Let the tomato skins dry out slowly for several hours, checking periodically, until they are completely dry and crisp.
Grind into Powder: Once the tomato skins are fully dehydrated and brittle, remove them from the oven or dehydrator and let them cool completely. Transfer the dried tomato skins to a spice grinder, blender, or food processor.
Pulse into Powder: Pulse the dried tomato skins in the grinder or blender until they are ground into a fine powder. You may need to shake or stir the powder occasionally to ensure even grinding.
Store in an Airtight Container: Transfer the tomato skin powder to an airtight container, such as a glass jar or a sealed plastic bag. Store it in a cool, dry place away from heat and moisture.

Usage:

- Use tomato skin powder as a seasoning or flavoring agent in soups, stews, sauces, pasta dishes, or any recipe where you want to add a concentrated tomato flavor.
- Sprinkle tomato skin powder over roasted vegetables, salads, or popcorn for a savory twist.
- Mix tomato skin powder with salt, pepper, and other herbs/spices to create a custom seasoning blend.

Tomato skin powder is a versatile ingredient that can add depth of flavor and richness to your cooking. Experiment with different ways to incorporate it into your favorite dishes and enjoy the unique taste of homemade tomato skin powder!

Celery Leaf Salad

Ingredients:

- Celery leaves (from 1 bunch of celery)
- 1 cucumber, thinly sliced
- 1 small red onion, thinly sliced
- Cherry tomatoes, halved
- Feta cheese, crumbled (optional)
- Kalamata olives, pitted (optional)
- Lemon vinaigrette (see recipe below)
- Salt and pepper, to taste

For Lemon Vinaigrette:

- 1/4 cup extra-virgin olive oil
- 2 tablespoons fresh lemon juice
- 1 teaspoon Dijon mustard
- 1 clove garlic, minced
- Salt and pepper, to taste

Instructions:

Prepare Celery Leaves: Wash the celery leaves thoroughly under cold water to remove any dirt or debris. Pat them dry with a clean kitchen towel or paper towels. Separate the leaves from the stalks and discard any tough stems.
Make Lemon Vinaigrette: In a small bowl, whisk together the olive oil, lemon juice, Dijon mustard, minced garlic, salt, and pepper until well combined. Adjust the seasoning to your taste.
Assemble Salad: In a large salad bowl, combine the celery leaves, thinly sliced cucumber, red onion, and halved cherry tomatoes. If using, add crumbled feta cheese and pitted Kalamata olives for extra flavor.
Add Lemon Vinaigrette: Drizzle the lemon vinaigrette over the salad ingredients, tossing gently to coat everything evenly. Start with a small amount of dressing and add more as needed.
Season with Salt and Pepper: Taste the salad and season with additional salt and pepper if desired.
Serve: Transfer the celery leaf salad to serving plates or bowls. Garnish with additional celery leaves or fresh herbs if desired.

Optional Additions: Feel free to customize the salad by adding other ingredients like avocado slices, cooked chickpeas, grilled chicken, or nuts/seeds for added texture and protein.

Celery leaf salad is best served fresh and makes a wonderful side dish or light lunch. It's a great way to enjoy the flavor and crunch of celery leaves in a delicious and nutritious salad. Enjoy!

Orange Peel Vinegar

Ingredients:

- Orange peels (from 2-3 oranges)
- White vinegar or apple cider vinegar

Instructions:

Prepare Orange Peels: Wash the oranges thoroughly under cold water to remove any dirt or residues. Use a vegetable peeler or knife to peel the oranges, removing only the outer colored zest while avoiding the bitter white pith underneath. Cut the peels into smaller pieces if desired.
Dry the Orange Peels (Optional): If you have time, you can let the orange peels air-dry for a few hours to reduce moisture content. This step is optional but can help intensify the citrus aroma during infusion.
Place in a Glass Jar: Place the orange peels in a clean glass jar or container with a tight-fitting lid.
Cover with Vinegar: Pour white vinegar or apple cider vinegar over the orange peels, ensuring that they are fully submerged in the vinegar. Fill the jar almost to the top, leaving a small amount of space at the top.
Infuse: Seal the jar tightly with the lid and store it in a cool, dark place for about 2-3 weeks to allow the orange peels to infuse into the vinegar. Shake the jar gently every few days to agitate the mixture and promote infusion.
Strain the Vinegar: After 2-3 weeks, strain the infused vinegar through a fine-mesh sieve or cheesecloth into a clean container to remove the orange peels and any sediment.
Store: Transfer the orange peel vinegar to a clean bottle or jar with a lid for storage. Store it in a cool, dark place away from direct sunlight.

Uses for Orange Peel Vinegar:

- Cleaning: Orange peel vinegar can be used as a natural and effective cleaner for various surfaces, including countertops, sinks, glass, and floors. Dilute it with water (about 1:1 ratio) in a spray bottle and use it as an all-purpose cleaner.
- Cooking: Use orange peel vinegar in salad dressings, marinades, sauces, and vinaigrettes to add a subtle citrus flavor to your dishes.
- Household Deodorizer: Orange peel vinegar can help neutralize odors in your home. Place a small bowl of vinegar in a room to absorb unwanted smells.

- Beauty and Skincare: Add a splash of orange peel vinegar to your bathwater for a refreshing and aromatic soak. It can also be used as a facial toner (diluted with water) to help balance skin pH and tighten pores.

Homemade orange peel vinegar is a versatile and eco-friendly alternative to commercial cleaning products and culinary ingredients. Enjoy experimenting with this citrus-infused vinegar in various ways around your home!

Pineapple Core Jam

Ingredients:

- Core of 1 pineapple, chopped into small pieces
- 1 cup granulated sugar (adjust to taste)
- Juice of 1 lemon
- 1/2 cup water
- Optional: 1 tablespoon rum or coconut rum (for flavor)

Instructions:

Prepare Pineapple Core: Remove the skin and crown of the pineapple. Cut the pineapple into quarters lengthwise, and then cut out the tough core from each quarter. Chop the pineapple core into small pieces.

Cook Pineapple Core: In a medium saucepan, combine the chopped pineapple core pieces, sugar, lemon juice, and water. Bring the mixture to a boil over medium-high heat, stirring occasionally.

Simmer: Once boiling, reduce the heat to medium-low and let the mixture simmer for about 30-40 minutes, or until the pineapple core pieces are tender and the mixture has thickened into a jam-like consistency. Stir occasionally to prevent sticking and burning.

Check Consistency: To test if the jam is ready, place a small amount on a chilled plate. If it sets and wrinkles slightly when you push it with your finger, it's done.

Add Rum (Optional): If using rum or coconut rum for flavor, stir it into the jam during the last few minutes of cooking.

Cool and Store: Remove the saucepan from the heat and let the pineapple core jam cool slightly. Transfer the jam to clean, sterilized jars or containers. Allow it to cool completely before sealing the jars.

Enjoy: Spread the pineapple core jam on toast, biscuits, or use it as a topping for yogurt, pancakes, or desserts. It's also a delightful filling for pastries and cakes.

Storage: Store the pineapple core jam in the refrigerator for up to several weeks. If you prefer longer storage, you can process the jars in a water bath for canning following safe canning practices.

Pineapple core jam is a wonderful way to reduce food waste and enjoy a unique tropical-flavored spread. Feel free to adjust the sweetness and flavorings according to your taste preferences. Enjoy your homemade pineapple core jam!

Coffee Ground Body Scrub

Ingredients:

- 1/2 cup used coffee grounds (cooled)
- 1/4 cup granulated sugar or sea salt (for additional exfoliation)
- 1/4 cup coconut oil, almond oil, olive oil, or any other carrier oil of your choice
- Optional: a few drops of essential oil (such as lavender, peppermint, or vanilla) for fragrance

Instructions:

Collect Coffee Grounds: After brewing your coffee, allow the used coffee grounds to cool down completely.

Mix Ingredients: In a mixing bowl, combine the cooled coffee grounds with granulated sugar or sea salt. The sugar or salt will enhance the exfoliating effect of the scrub.

Add Oil: Pour the coconut oil, almond oil, or your chosen carrier oil into the bowl with the coffee grounds and sugar/salt. Mix well until all the ingredients are thoroughly combined. The oil will moisturize and nourish your skin.

Add Essential Oil (Optional): If you want to add a pleasant fragrance to your scrub, incorporate a few drops of essential oil of your choice into the mixture. Stir well to distribute the essential oil evenly.

Adjust Consistency: If the scrub seems too dry, you can add a bit more oil until you reach your desired consistency. If it's too oily, add a little more coffee grounds or sugar/salt.

Store in a Jar: Transfer the coffee ground body scrub into a clean, airtight container or jar with a lid.

How to Use:

- In the shower or bath, scoop out a small amount of the coffee ground body scrub using clean fingers or a spoon.
- Gently massage the scrub onto damp skin in circular motions, focusing on areas where you want to exfoliate (such as elbows, knees, heels, and thighs).
- Rinse off thoroughly with warm water.
- Pat your skin dry with a towel and follow up with a moisturizer if needed.

Tips:

- Use the coffee ground body scrub 1-2 times per week for smooth and radiant skin.
- Avoid using the scrub on broken or irritated skin.
- Store the scrub in a cool, dry place between uses to prevent spoilage.
- Experiment with different oils and essential oils to customize the scent and benefits of your coffee ground body scrub.

Enjoy the invigorating experience and silky-smooth skin after using this DIY coffee ground body scrub!

Leftover Vegetable Stir Fry

Ingredients:

- Leftover vegetable stir fry (already cooked and seasoned)
- Cooked rice or noodles (for serving)
- Soy sauce or tamari, to taste
- Optional toppings: chopped green onions, sesame seeds, crushed peanuts, or sliced chili peppers

Instructions:

Prepare Your Ingredients: Ensure that you have your leftover vegetable stir fry ready to be reheated and your choice of cooked rice or noodles for serving.
Heat a Pan or Wok: Place a large pan or wok over medium heat. Add a small amount of oil (such as vegetable oil or sesame oil) if needed.
Reheat the Stir Fry: Transfer the leftover vegetable stir fry into the heated pan or wok. Stir and toss the vegetables to evenly distribute them in the pan.
Add Soy Sauce or Tamari: Drizzle soy sauce or tamari over the vegetables according to your taste preference. This will add flavor and enhance the seasoning of the stir fry.
Stir and Heat Through: Continue to stir and cook the leftover vegetable stir fry until it is heated through. The vegetables should be tender and hot.
Serve Over Rice or Noodles: Place a serving of cooked rice or noodles on a plate or in a bowl. Spoon the reheated vegetable stir fry over the rice or noodles.
Add Optional Toppings: Garnish your leftover vegetable stir fry with chopped green onions, sesame seeds, crushed peanuts, or sliced chili peppers for added flavor and texture.
Enjoy Your Meal: Your leftover vegetable stir fry is now ready to be enjoyed! Serve immediately while it's hot.

Tips for Leftover Vegetable Stir Fry:

- Feel free to add protein: If you want to make your leftover stir fry more substantial, you can add cooked chicken, tofu, shrimp, or beef strips.
- Customize the seasoning: Adjust the flavor of your stir fry by adding more soy sauce, a splash of rice vinegar, or a sprinkle of garlic powder or ginger powder.
- Use up any leftover vegetables: Leftover stir fry is a great way to use up any vegetables you have on hand, such as bell peppers, broccoli, carrots, snap peas, or mushrooms.

- Make it spicy: If you like heat, add a drizzle of sriracha sauce or red chili flakes to spice up your leftover vegetable stir fry.

Leftover vegetable stir fry is a versatile and satisfying meal that can be tailored to your taste preferences. It's a quick and easy way to enjoy a nutritious dish using leftovers from the fridge!

Corn Husk Tamales

Ingredients:

For the Masa Dough:

- 2 cups masa harina (corn flour for tamales)
- 1 1/4 cups warm water or broth
- 1/2 cup lard or vegetable shortening (or substitute with softened butter for a vegetarian option)
- 1 teaspoon baking powder
- 1 teaspoon salt

For the Filling (Suggested):

- Shredded cooked chicken or pork (for savory tamales)
- Cheese and green chilies (for vegetarian tamales)
- Sweetened corn or fruit (for sweet tamales)

For Assembling:

- Dried corn husks, soaked in warm water until pliable
- Salsa or hot sauce, for serving (optional)

Instructions:

Prepare Corn Husks: Place the dried corn husks in a large bowl or baking dish and cover them with warm water. Allow them to soak for at least 30 minutes, or until they are soft and pliable. Drain and pat dry with a clean towel.

Make Masa Dough: In a mixing bowl, combine the masa harina, warm water or broth, lard or vegetable shortening, baking powder, and salt. Mix well until you have a soft and slightly sticky dough. The dough should hold together and spread easily.

Assemble Tamales:

- Take a soaked corn husk and spread a thin layer of masa dough (about 1-2 tablespoons) evenly over the center of the husk, leaving a border along the edges.
- Place a spoonful of your chosen filling (such as shredded meat, cheese, or sweet filling) in the center of the masa dough.

Fold and Tie Tamales:

- Fold the sides of the corn husk over the masa and filling to enclose them completely.

- Fold up the bottom of the husk to seal the tamale, then tie it closed with a thin strip of corn husk or kitchen twine.

Steam Tamales:
- Arrange the tamales upright in a steamer basket or pot with a steamer insert.
- Add water to the bottom of the pot, making sure the water level is below the steamer insert.
- Cover the tamales with a layer of extra corn husks or a clean kitchen towel to trap steam.
- Steam the tamales over medium heat for about 1.5 to 2 hours, or until the masa is cooked through and firm.

Serve:
- Allow the tamales to cool slightly before unwrapping them.
- Serve the tamales warm, with salsa or hot sauce on the side if desired.

Tips for Corn Husk Tamales:

- Customize your fillings: You can get creative with the fillings for your tamales. Try using different meats, cheeses, vegetables, or sweet fillings like chocolate or fruit.
- Make ahead: Tamales can be assembled and wrapped in advance, then steamed just before serving. They also freeze well for longer storage.
- Use fresh masa if available: While masa harina is convenient and widely available, using freshly prepared masa can result in even more flavorful tamales.

Enjoy these homemade corn husk tamales as a delicious and satisfying dish that's perfect for sharing with family and friends!

Watermelon Seed Butter

Ingredients:

- Raw watermelon seeds (from a fresh watermelon)
- Optional: Salt, honey, or sweetener of your choice (to taste)

Instructions:

Collect Watermelon Seeds: Remove the seeds from a fresh watermelon. Rinse them thoroughly under cold water to remove any remaining fruit pieces or debris.
Dry the Seeds: Spread the cleaned watermelon seeds out on a baking sheet in a single layer. Let them air dry for a few hours or overnight until they are completely dry. Alternatively, you can roast the seeds in the oven at a low temperature (around 275°F or 135°C) for about 15-20 minutes to dry them out.
Roast the Seeds (Optional): For a deeper flavor, you can roast the dried watermelon seeds in the oven at 275°F (135°C) for about 15-20 minutes until they are lightly golden and fragrant. Allow them to cool before proceeding.
Blend the Seeds: Transfer the dried (or roasted) watermelon seeds to a high-speed blender or food processor. Blend the seeds on high speed, scraping down the sides as needed, until they start to break down and release their oils.
Continue Blending: Keep blending the seeds until they form a smooth and creamy butter consistency. This process may take several minutes, depending on the power of your blender or processor.
Add Optional Ingredients: If desired, add a pinch of salt, honey, or your preferred sweetener to the seed butter and blend again until well combined. Taste and adjust the flavor as needed.
Store in a Jar: Transfer the watermelon seed butter to a clean glass jar or airtight container. Store it in the refrigerator for freshness.

Usage:

- Enjoy watermelon seed butter as a spread on toast, pancakes, or waffles.
- Use it as a dip for fruit slices or veggie sticks.
- Incorporate it into smoothies, oatmeal, or yogurt bowls for added protein and flavor.

Watermelon seed butter is a nutritious and delicious alternative to nut butters,

especially for those with nut allergies or dietary restrictions. It's packed with nutrients and can be used in various ways to enhance your meals and snacks. Experiment with different flavors and enjoy the benefits of homemade watermelon seed butter!

Apple Peel Tea

Ingredients:

- Apple peels (from 2-3 apples)
- 4 cups of water
- Optional: Cinnamon sticks, cloves, ginger slices, or lemon slices for added flavor

Instructions:

Wash the Apples: Start by thoroughly washing the apples under cold water to remove any dirt or residues from the peels.
Peel the Apples: Use a vegetable peeler or knife to carefully remove the peels from the apples. Try to remove only the outer colored part of the peel, leaving behind the inner flesh.
Boil the Water: In a medium-sized saucepan, bring 4 cups of water to a boil over high heat.
Add Apple Peels: Once the water is boiling, add the apple peels to the saucepan. If desired, you can also add optional flavorings such as cinnamon sticks, cloves, ginger slices, or lemon slices to enhance the flavor of the tea.
Simmer: Reduce the heat to low and let the apple peels simmer in the water for about 10-15 minutes. This will allow the flavors and nutrients from the peels to infuse into the water.
Strain the Tea: After simmering, remove the saucepan from the heat. Use a fine-mesh sieve or tea strainer to strain the tea, separating the liquid (tea) from the apple peels and any other flavorings.
Serve: Pour the apple peel tea into cups or mugs. You can enjoy it as is or sweeten it with honey, maple syrup, or another sweetener of your choice.
Optional: Chill and Serve Iced: For a refreshing iced tea, let the apple peel tea cool to room temperature and then refrigerate until chilled. Serve over ice with a slice of lemon or a sprig of mint.

Tips for Apple Peel Tea:

- Use organic apples if possible to avoid pesticide residues on the peels.
- Experiment with different spices and flavorings to customize the taste of your apple peel tea.
- Apple peel tea can be enjoyed hot or cold, depending on your preference and the weather.

Apple peel tea is a comforting and nutritious beverage that can be enjoyed any time of day. It's a wonderful way to make use of apple peels and benefit from their natural goodness. Sip and savor this homemade tea for a delightful apple-infused experience!

Onion Skin Dye

Ingredients and Materials:

- Onion skins (skins from yellow onions, red onions, or a mix of both)
- Water
- White fabric or eggs (pre-washed and dampened)
- Stainless steel or enamel pot
- Strainer or colander
- Rubber gloves (optional, to protect hands from dye)

Instructions:

Collect Onion Skins: Save up the dry outer skins of onions from cooking. You can also ask for onion skins at grocery stores or farmers' markets.
Prepare Fabric or Eggs: If using fabric, wash it thoroughly to remove any dirt or residues. For eggs, make sure they are clean and dampened before dyeing.
Boil Onion Skins: Place the onion skins in a stainless steel or enamel pot and cover them with water. Use approximately 1 cup of onion skins for every 4 cups of water, or adjust based on the intensity of color desired.
Simmer the Mixture: Bring the water and onion skins to a boil, then reduce the heat and let it simmer for about 30 minutes to 1 hour. The longer you simmer, the deeper the color will be.
Strain the Dye: Once you achieve the desired color, remove the pot from the heat and let the mixture cool slightly. Strain the dye liquid through a strainer or colander to remove the onion skins, leaving you with a clear dye solution.
Dye Fabric or Eggs: Submerge the pre-washed fabric or dampened eggs into the strained dye liquid. For lighter colors, leave them in the dye bath for a shorter time (e.g., 30 minutes). For deeper colors, leave them in the dye bath for a longer time (e.g., several hours or overnight).
Rinse and Dry: After dyeing, remove the fabric or eggs from the dye bath and rinse them under cold water until the water runs clear. Hang the fabric to air dry or gently pat dry the eggs with a towel.

Tips for Onion Skin Dyeing:

- Experiment with different types of onion skins (yellow, red, or a mix) to achieve a variety of colors.
- For a more vibrant color, use a mordant like vinegar or salt to help set the dye.

- Add decorative patterns to your fabric or eggs by tying them with rubber bands or using wax resist techniques before dyeing.
- Store any leftover onion skin dye in a sealed container in the refrigerator for future use.

Onion skin dyeing is a natural and eco-friendly way to create beautiful, earthy colors on fabric or eggs. Have fun experimenting with different materials and techniques to achieve unique and artistic results!

Bell Pepper Seed Hummus

Ingredients:

- Bell pepper seeds (seeds from 2-3 bell peppers)
- 1 can (15 oz) chickpeas, drained and rinsed
- 2-3 tablespoons tahini (sesame paste)
- 2-3 cloves garlic, minced
- Juice of 1 lemon
- 2-3 tablespoons olive oil
- Salt and pepper, to taste
- Water, as needed

Instructions:

Collect Bell Pepper Seeds: Remove the seeds from 2-3 bell peppers. Rinse the seeds under cold water to remove any flesh or debris.

Dry the Seeds: Spread the bell pepper seeds out on a baking sheet and let them air dry for a few hours or overnight until they are completely dry.

Roast the Seeds (Optional): For enhanced flavor, you can roast the dried bell pepper seeds in the oven at 350°F (175°C) for about 10-15 minutes until they are golden brown and fragrant. Let them cool before using.

Prepare Hummus Base: In a food processor, combine the chickpeas, tahini, minced garlic, lemon juice, olive oil, salt, and pepper.

Add Bell Pepper Seeds: Add the dried or roasted bell pepper seeds to the food processor.

Blend Until Smooth: Process the mixture until smooth and creamy, scraping down the sides of the food processor as needed. If the hummus is too thick, add water a tablespoon at a time until you reach your desired consistency.

Adjust Seasonings: Taste the hummus and adjust the seasonings to your preference. Add more lemon juice, salt, or pepper as needed.

Serve and Enjoy: Transfer the bell pepper seed hummus to a serving bowl. Drizzle with a little extra olive oil and garnish with additional bell pepper seeds or fresh herbs if desired. Serve with pita bread, crackers, or fresh vegetables.

Tips for Bell Pepper Seed Hummus:

- Customize the flavor: Feel free to add spices or herbs like cumin, paprika, or parsley to enhance the flavor of the hummus.

- Experiment with other seeds: You can also try using seeds from other vegetables like squash, pumpkin, or cucumber for different variations of seed hummus.
- Store leftovers: Keep the hummus refrigerated in an airtight container for up to 4-5 days. Stir well before serving.

Bell pepper seed hummus is a nutritious and flavorful dip that's perfect for snacking or serving as an appetizer. Enjoy this unique twist on traditional hummus using edible bell pepper seeds!

Lemon Rind Sorbet

Ingredients:

- 1 cup granulated sugar
- 1 cup water
- Zest of 2-3 lemons
- 1 cup freshly squeezed lemon juice (from about 4-5 lemons)
- 2 cups cold water

Instructions:

Make Simple Syrup:
- In a saucepan, combine the granulated sugar, 1 cup of water, and lemon zest.
- Heat over medium heat, stirring occasionally, until the sugar is completely dissolved.
- Once the sugar is dissolved, remove the saucepan from the heat and let the simple syrup cool to room temperature.

Prepare Lemon Juice:
- While the simple syrup is cooling, juice the lemons to get 1 cup of fresh lemon juice.

Combine Ingredients:
- In a large bowl, mix together the cooled simple syrup (including the lemon zest) and the freshly squeezed lemon juice.
- Stir in 2 cups of cold water to dilute the mixture. Adjust the amount of water to taste, depending on how tart you prefer your sorbet.

Chill the Mixture:
- Cover the bowl with plastic wrap and refrigerate the lemon mixture for at least 2-3 hours, or until thoroughly chilled.

Churn in Ice Cream Maker:
- Once the lemon mixture is chilled, pour it into an ice cream maker and churn according to the manufacturer's instructions. This usually takes about 20-30 minutes, or until the sorbet reaches a slushy, frozen consistency.

Freeze:
- Transfer the churned lemon sorbet into a freezer-safe container.
- Cover the container with a lid or plastic wrap and freeze the sorbet for an additional 2-3 hours, or until it firms up to a scoopable consistency.

Serve:

- Scoop the lemon rind sorbet into bowls or cones.
- Garnish with fresh mint leaves or lemon zest for an extra burst of flavor.

Tips for Lemon Rind Sorbet:

- For a smoother texture, strain the lemon mixture through a fine-mesh sieve before churning to remove the lemon zest.
- Adjust the sweetness by adding more or less sugar according to your taste preferences.
- Experiment with other citrus fruits like lime or orange to create different variations of sorbet.
- To make sorbet without an ice cream maker, pour the chilled lemon mixture into a shallow pan. Place it in the freezer and use a fork to scrape and stir the mixture every 30 minutes until it reaches the desired consistency.

Enjoy this homemade lemon rind sorbet as a light and refreshing dessert on a hot day or after a flavorful meal. The natural citrus zest adds a delightful twist to classic sorbet!

Carrot Top Chimichurri

Ingredients:

- 1 cup carrot tops (greens), washed and dried
- 1/2 cup fresh parsley leaves
- 2-3 cloves garlic, minced
- 1 shallot, finely chopped
- 1/4 cup red wine vinegar or apple cider vinegar
- 1/2 cup olive oil
- 1 teaspoon dried oregano
- 1/2 teaspoon red pepper flakes (adjust to taste)
- Salt and black pepper, to taste

Instructions:

Prepare Carrot Tops: Remove the carrot tops (greens) from a bunch of fresh carrots. Wash them thoroughly under cold water to remove any dirt or debris. Pat dry with a clean kitchen towel or paper towels.
Blend Ingredients: In a food processor or blender, combine the carrot tops, parsley leaves, minced garlic, chopped shallot, red wine vinegar (or apple cider vinegar), olive oil, dried oregano, and red pepper flakes.
Blend Until Smooth: Pulse or blend the ingredients until you achieve a smooth and well-combined sauce. You may need to scrape down the sides of the processor or blender and blend again to ensure everything is incorporated.
Season to Taste: Taste the chimichurri and season with salt and black pepper according to your preference. Adjust the amount of red pepper flakes for desired spiciness.
Serve or Store: Transfer the carrot top chimichurri to a bowl or jar with a lid. You can use it immediately as a sauce or marinade for grilled meats, roasted vegetables, or as a topping for fish or poultry. Alternatively, store the chimichurri in the refrigerator for up to one week.

Serving Suggestions for Carrot Top Chimichurri:

- Use as a sauce for grilled steak, chicken, or seafood.
- Drizzle over roasted vegetables or potatoes.
- Spread on sandwiches or wraps for extra flavor.
- Mix into pasta salads or grain bowls.
- Serve as a dip for bread or crudité.

Carrot top chimichurri is a versatile and delicious condiment that adds freshness and herbaceous flavor to a variety of dishes. It's a wonderful way to reduce food waste by using every part of the carrot. Enjoy experimenting with this homemade carrot top chimichurri and discover new ways to incorporate it into your meals!

Broccoli Stem Soup

Ingredients:

- 2-3 broccoli stems, peeled and chopped
- 1 tablespoon olive oil or butter
- 1 onion, chopped
- 2 cloves garlic, minced
- 1 potato, peeled and diced (optional, for added creaminess)
- 4 cups vegetable broth or chicken broth
- Salt and pepper, to taste
- Optional toppings: chopped fresh herbs (such as parsley or chives), grated cheese, or a dollop of Greek yogurt

Instructions:

Prepare Broccoli Stems: Peel the tough outer skin of the broccoli stems using a vegetable peeler. Chop the peeled broccoli stems into small pieces.
Sauté Onion and Garlic: In a large pot or Dutch oven, heat olive oil or butter over medium heat. Add chopped onion and minced garlic. Sauté for 3-4 minutes, or until the onion becomes translucent and fragrant.
Add Broccoli Stems: Add the chopped broccoli stems (and diced potato, if using) to the pot. Sauté for another 2-3 minutes, stirring occasionally.
Add Broth and Simmer: Pour in the vegetable or chicken broth to cover the vegetables. Bring the mixture to a boil, then reduce the heat to low. Cover the pot and simmer for about 15-20 minutes, or until the broccoli stems and potatoes (if using) are tender.
Blend the Soup: Using an immersion blender or regular blender, carefully blend the soup until smooth and creamy. If using a regular blender, work in batches and be cautious of hot liquid.
Season and Adjust: Taste the soup and season with salt and pepper according to your preference. Add more broth or water if the soup is too thick.
Serve: Ladle the broccoli stem soup into bowls. Garnish with chopped fresh herbs, grated cheese, or a dollop of Greek yogurt if desired.

Tips for Broccoli Stem Soup:

- Use homemade broth for the best flavor, or use low-sodium store-bought broth.
- Feel free to customize the soup by adding other vegetables like cauliflower, celery, or spinach.

- For added richness, stir in a splash of cream or coconut milk at the end of cooking.
- Store leftover soup in an airtight container in the refrigerator for up to 3-4 days, or freeze for longer storage.

Broccoli stem soup is a comforting and nutritious dish that's perfect for lunch or dinner. It's a great way to reduce food waste and enjoy the wholesome flavors of broccoli stems. Serve this soup with crusty bread or a side salad for a satisfying meal!

Cucumber Peel Salad

Ingredients:

- Peels from 2-3 large cucumbers
- 1 large tomato, diced
- 1/4 red onion, thinly sliced
- 1/4 cup chopped fresh parsley or cilantro
- Juice of 1 lemon
- 2 tablespoons olive oil
- Salt and pepper, to taste
- Optional: crumbled feta cheese, olives, or diced bell peppers for additional flavor

Instructions:

Prepare Cucumber Peels: Wash the cucumbers thoroughly under cold water. Use a vegetable peeler to peel the cucumbers, creating long strips of cucumber peels. You can also use a knife to carefully slice the cucumbers into thin strips if preferred.
Combine Ingredients: In a large salad bowl, combine the cucumber peels, diced tomato, thinly sliced red onion, and chopped fresh parsley or cilantro.
Make Dressing: In a small bowl or jar, whisk together the lemon juice, olive oil, salt, and pepper to make the dressing.
Toss Salad: Pour the dressing over the cucumber peel mixture in the salad bowl. Toss everything together gently to coat the ingredients with the dressing.
Add Optional Ingredients: If desired, add crumbled feta cheese, olives, or diced bell peppers to the salad for extra flavor and texture.
Chill and Serve: Cover the salad bowl and refrigerate for at least 15-30 minutes to allow the flavors to meld together.
Serve: Serve the cucumber peel salad chilled as a side dish or appetizer. Enjoy its crisp and refreshing taste!

Tips for Cucumber Peel Salad:

- Use English cucumbers or other thin-skinned cucumbers for the best texture and flavor of the peels.
- Add a pinch of dried herbs like oregano or dill to the dressing for extra seasoning.
- Customize the salad by adding other fresh vegetables or herbs based on what you have on hand.
- This salad pairs well with grilled meats, seafood, or as part of a vegetarian meal.

- Make sure to wash the cucumbers thoroughly before peeling to remove any dirt or residues.

Cucumber peel salad is a simple and healthy dish that celebrates the natural flavors of cucumbers. It's a great way to reduce food waste and enjoy a light and crunchy salad with minimal effort. Serve this salad at picnics, barbecues, or alongside your favorite meals!

Sweet Potato Skin Chips

Ingredients:

- Sweet potato skins (from 2-3 sweet potatoes), washed and dried
- 2 tablespoons olive oil or melted coconut oil
- Salt, to taste
- Optional seasonings: garlic powder, paprika, cayenne pepper, or any other desired spices

Instructions:

Prepare Sweet Potato Skins: Wash the sweet potatoes thoroughly under cold water to remove any dirt or residues. Use a vegetable peeler or knife to remove the skins, leaving a thin layer of flesh on the skins.

Cut into Strips: Lay the sweet potato skins flat on a cutting board. Use a sharp knife to cut them into thin strips or chip-like shapes.

Toss with Oil and Seasonings: In a bowl, toss the sweet potato skin strips with olive oil or melted coconut oil until they are evenly coated. Sprinkle with salt and any desired seasonings, such as garlic powder, paprika, or cayenne pepper, for added flavor.

Bake in the Oven:
- Preheat your oven to 400°F (200°C).
- Line a baking sheet with parchment paper or aluminum foil for easy cleanup.
- Arrange the seasoned sweet potato skin strips in a single layer on the baking sheet, ensuring they are not overlapping.

Bake Until Crispy:
- Place the baking sheet in the preheated oven and bake for 15-20 minutes, or until the sweet potato skins are crispy and golden brown.
- Check and stir the skins halfway through baking to ensure even cooking.

Cool and Enjoy: Remove the sweet potato skin chips from the oven and let them cool slightly on the baking sheet. They will continue to crisp up as they cool.

Serve: Transfer the sweet potato skin chips to a serving bowl or plate. Enjoy them as a crunchy and flavorful snack!

Tips for Sweet Potato Skin Chips:

- Use organic sweet potatoes if possible, especially since you'll be eating the skins.

- Experiment with different seasonings to create various flavor profiles. Try using smoked paprika, chili powder, or ranch seasoning.
- Store any leftover sweet potato skin chips in an airtight container at room temperature for a few days. Re-crisp them in a toaster oven or low-temperature oven if they become soft.

Sweet potato skin chips are a nutritious and tasty snack that's perfect for munching on while watching a movie or as a side dish with sandwiches or burgers. They're a great way to reduce food waste and enjoy every part of the sweet potato!

Citrus Peel Infused Oil

Ingredients:

- Zest from 2-3 organic citrus fruits (such as lemons, oranges, limes, or grapefruits)
- 1 cup olive oil or another neutral oil (e.g., grapeseed oil, sunflower oil)
- Optional: Whole dried spices like peppercorns, coriander seeds, or dried herbs like rosemary or thyme

Instructions:

Prepare Citrus Zest:
- Wash the citrus fruits thoroughly to remove any wax or residues. Use a vegetable peeler or zester to carefully remove the colored outer zest (avoid the bitter white pith underneath).

Dry the Zest:
- Lay the citrus zest strips on a paper towel and let them air dry for about 1-2 hours. This helps to remove excess moisture.

Infuse the Oil:
- In a clean glass jar or bottle, combine the dried citrus zest with the olive oil or neutral oil of your choice.
- Optionally, add a small handful of whole dried spices or herbs for additional flavor. This step is entirely optional but can enhance the infused oil.

Let it Infuse:
- Seal the jar or bottle tightly and place it in a cool, dark place (such as a pantry or cupboard) to infuse for at least 1 week. The longer you let it infuse, the stronger the citrus flavor will be.

Strain the Oil:
- After the infusion period, strain the infused oil through a fine-mesh sieve or cheesecloth to remove the citrus zest and any added spices or herbs. Squeeze the zest to extract as much flavored oil as possible.

Transfer and Store:
- Pour the strained citrus peel-infused oil into a clean glass bottle or jar with a tight-fitting lid.
- Label the bottle with the type of infused oil and the date it was made.
- Store the infused oil in a cool, dark place (such as the refrigerator) to preserve its freshness and flavor.

Tips for Citrus Peel-Infused Oil:

- Use organic citrus fruits to avoid pesticides or wax on the peel.
- Experiment with different combinations of citrus zest and spices/herbs to create unique flavor profiles.
- Try using the infused oil in salad dressings, marinades for chicken or fish, drizzled over grilled vegetables, or as a finishing touch on pasta dishes.
- Infused oil can be stored for several weeks to a few months, depending on storage conditions. Discard if you notice any signs of spoilage or rancidity.

Citrus peel-infused oil adds a delightful burst of citrus flavor to your cooking and can elevate a wide range of dishes. Enjoy the freshness and versatility of homemade infused oil in your kitchen!

Herb Stem Infused Vinegar

Ingredients:

- Herb stems (e.g., parsley, cilantro, basil, thyme, rosemary, dill, etc.)
- White wine vinegar or apple cider vinegar

Instructions:

Collect Herb Stems:
- Save leftover herb stems from fresh herbs that you have used in cooking or meal preparation. Rinse them under cold water to remove any dirt or debris.

Prepare Herb Stems:
- Trim off any discolored or tough parts from the herb stems. Keep the tender parts and leaves intact.

Choose Vinegar:
- Select a good-quality white wine vinegar or apple cider vinegar for the infusion. The vinegar should have a mild flavor to allow the herb aromas to shine through.

Combine Herb Stems and Vinegar:
- Place the cleaned and trimmed herb stems into a clean glass jar or bottle.
- Pour the white wine vinegar or apple cider vinegar over the herb stems, covering them completely.

Infuse the Vinegar:
- Seal the jar or bottle tightly with a lid.
- Place the infused vinegar in a cool, dark place (such as a pantry or cupboard) to infuse for at least 1-2 weeks. The longer you let it infuse, the stronger the herb flavor will be.

Strain and Store:
- After the infusion period, strain the herb stem-infused vinegar through a fine-mesh sieve or cheesecloth to remove the herb stems and any sediment.
- Transfer the infused vinegar into a clean glass bottle or jar with a tight-fitting lid for storage.

Label and Use:
- Label the bottle with the type of infused vinegar and the date it was made.
- Use the herb stem-infused vinegar in salad dressings, marinades, sauces, or as a flavorful addition to homemade vinaigrettes.

Tips for Herb Stem-Infused Vinegar:

- Combine different herb stems to create unique flavor combinations.
- Use herb stem-infused vinegar to add depth of flavor to pickles or preserved vegetables.
- Store the infused vinegar in a cool, dark place to preserve its flavor and color.
- Experiment with various vinegar types and herb combinations to suit your taste preferences.

Herb stem-infused vinegar is a simple yet effective way to reduce food waste and enhance the flavors of your dishes with minimal effort. Enjoy the fresh herbal essence of homemade infused vinegar in your culinary creations!

Banana Peel Vegan Bacon

Ingredients:

- Peels from 2-3 ripe bananas (make sure they are organic for safety)
- 2 tablespoons soy sauce or tamari
- 1 tablespoon maple syrup or agave nectar
- 1 tablespoon apple cider vinegar
- 1/2 teaspoon smoked paprika
- 1/4 teaspoon garlic powder
- Pinch of black pepper
- 1-2 tablespoons vegetable oil (for frying)

Instructions:

Prepare Banana Peels:
- Wash the bananas thoroughly under cold water to remove any dirt or residues. Carefully peel the bananas and set aside the fruit for another use (you only need the peels).

Remove Inner Fibers:
- Use a spoon or butter knife to scrape off the inner fibers from the banana peels. The peels should be relatively smooth on both sides.

Marinate the Peels:
- In a shallow dish or bowl, whisk together soy sauce (or tamari), maple syrup (or agave nectar), apple cider vinegar, smoked paprika, garlic powder, and black pepper.
- Add the banana peels to the marinade, ensuring they are well-coated. Let them marinate for at least 30 minutes, or ideally up to 2 hours, to absorb the flavors.

Cook the Banana Peels:
- Heat vegetable oil in a skillet over medium heat.
- Carefully add the marinated banana peels to the skillet in a single layer. Reserve the leftover marinade for later use.
- Cook the banana peels for 2-3 minutes on each side, or until they are crispy and caramelized. Use tongs to flip them gently.

Glaze with Marinade:
- Drizzle the leftover marinade over the banana peels while they are cooking in the skillet. This will add extra flavor and help create a caramelized coating.

Remove and Serve:

- Once the banana peel vegan bacon is crispy and golden brown, remove them from the skillet and place them on a plate lined with paper towels to absorb excess oil.
- Allow them to cool slightly before serving.

Enjoy:

- Serve banana peel vegan bacon as a crunchy snack, or use it as a plant-based bacon alternative in sandwiches, wraps, salads, or pasta dishes.

Tips for Banana Peel Vegan Bacon:

- Adjust the seasonings to suit your taste preferences. You can add more smoked paprika for a stronger smoky flavor, or increase the sweetness with additional maple syrup.
- Store any leftover banana peel vegan bacon in an airtight container in the refrigerator for up to 2-3 days. Reheat in a skillet or oven to restore crispiness before serving.
- Get creative with serving ideas! Try using banana peel vegan bacon in vegan BLT sandwiches, on avocado toast, or as a topping for vegan pizzas.

Banana peel vegan bacon is a fun and sustainable way to enjoy a plant-based version of a classic favorite. Experiment with different seasonings and enjoy the crispy, smoky goodness of this unique vegan snack!

Leftover Rice Fritters

Ingredients:

- 2 cups cooked leftover rice (white or brown)
- 1/2 cup grated cheese (cheddar, mozzarella, or your favorite melting cheese)
- 2 green onions, finely chopped
- 2 tablespoons chopped fresh parsley or cilantro
- 1/4 cup all-purpose flour
- 1/4 cup breadcrumbs (plus more for coating)
- 1/4 teaspoon garlic powder
- 1/4 teaspoon paprika
- Salt and pepper, to taste
- 1-2 eggs, beaten
- Vegetable oil, for frying

Instructions:

Prepare the Ingredients:
- In a mixing bowl, combine the cooked rice, grated cheese, chopped green onions, chopped parsley or cilantro, flour, breadcrumbs, garlic powder, paprika, salt, and pepper. Mix well to combine all the ingredients.

Form the Fritter Mixture:
- Add 1 beaten egg to the rice mixture and stir until everything is evenly combined. The mixture should hold together when squeezed. If needed, add another beaten egg to achieve the right consistency.

Shape the Fritters:
- Take a small handful of the rice mixture and shape it into a compact fritter or patty using your hands. Repeat with the remaining mixture to form all the fritters.

Coat the Fritters:
- Place some extra breadcrumbs on a plate. Gently coat each rice fritter in breadcrumbs, pressing lightly to adhere the breadcrumbs to the surface. This will help create a crispy crust when frying.

Fry the Fritters:
- In a large skillet or frying pan, heat vegetable oil over medium heat.
- Carefully add the rice fritters to the hot oil in batches, making sure not to overcrowd the pan.
- Fry the fritters for about 3-4 minutes on each side, or until they are golden brown and crispy. Use a spatula to flip them halfway through cooking.

Drain and Serve:
- Once cooked, transfer the rice fritters to a plate lined with paper towels to drain any excess oil.

Serve and Enjoy:
- Serve the leftover rice fritters warm as a snack or side dish. They are delicious on their own or with a dipping sauce like marinara, aioli, or yogurt-based dip.

Tips for Leftover Rice Fritters:

- Customize the fritters by adding other ingredients like finely chopped vegetables (such as bell peppers, corn, or peas), cooked crumbled bacon, or diced ham.
- Make sure the oil is hot enough before adding the fritters to ensure they become crispy and golden brown.
- Use gluten-free breadcrumbs and flour if you prefer a gluten-free version of these fritters.
- Store any leftover rice fritters in an airtight container in the refrigerator and reheat them in the oven or toaster oven to restore crispiness before serving.

Leftover rice fritters are a great way to transform plain rice into a delightful snack or meal. They are versatile, budget-friendly, and perfect for using up leftovers in a creative way. Enjoy making and eating these crispy rice fritters!

Veggie Scrap Quiche

Ingredients:

For the Quiche Filling:

- Assorted vegetable scraps (such as onion ends, carrot peels, broccoli stems, bell pepper cores, etc.)
- 1 tablespoon olive oil
- Salt and pepper, to taste
- 6 large eggs
- 1 cup milk or cream
- 1 cup shredded cheese (cheddar, Swiss, or any cheese of your choice)
- Herbs or spices (optional, such as parsley, thyme, or paprika)

For the Quiche Crust (optional, or use a pre-made crust):

- 1 1/4 cups all-purpose flour
- 1/2 teaspoon salt
- 1/2 cup cold unsalted butter, cubed
- 3-4 tablespoons ice water

Instructions:

Prepare the Vegetable Scraps:
- Collect assorted vegetable scraps such as onion ends, carrot peels, broccoli stems, and bell pepper cores. Wash them thoroughly under cold water.

Prep and Cook the Vegetable Scraps:
- Chop the vegetable scraps into small pieces.
- In a skillet, heat olive oil over medium heat. Add the chopped vegetable scraps and sauté until they are tender, about 5-7 minutes. Season with salt and pepper to taste. Set aside.

Make the Quiche Crust (optional):
- If making your own crust, combine flour and salt in a large bowl. Cut in cold butter using a pastry cutter or fork until the mixture resembles coarse crumbs.
- Gradually add ice water, 1 tablespoon at a time, and mix until dough starts to come together.

- Form dough into a ball, wrap in plastic wrap, and refrigerate for at least 30 minutes.
- Roll out the dough on a floured surface to fit a 9-inch pie dish. Press into the dish and trim the edges. Pre-bake the crust in a preheated oven at 375°F (190°C) for 10-12 minutes until lightly golden.

Prepare the Quiche Filling:
- In a mixing bowl, whisk together eggs, milk or cream, shredded cheese, and herbs or spices (if using). Season with salt and pepper.

Assemble and Bake the Quiche:
- Spread the sautéed vegetable scraps evenly over the pre-baked quiche crust (if using).
- Pour the egg mixture over the vegetables in the crust.
- Bake the quiche in the preheated oven at 375°F (190°C) for 30-35 minutes, or until the filling is set and the top is golden brown.
- Let the quiche cool slightly before slicing and serving.

Serve and Enjoy:
- Slice the veggie scrap quiche into wedges and serve warm or at room temperature. Enjoy as a main dish for brunch, lunch, or a light dinner.

Tips for Veggie Scrap Quiche:

- Use a variety of vegetable scraps for flavor and color variation.
- Feel free to add cooked meat (such as bacon, ham, or sausage) or additional cheese to the filling for extra protein.
- Customize the quiche with your favorite herbs and spices.
- Store any leftover quiche in the refrigerator and reheat slices in the microwave or oven before serving.

Veggie scrap quiche is a versatile and satisfying dish that transforms leftover vegetable scraps into a delicious meal. Get creative with your vegetable choices and enjoy this flavorful quiche for any occasion!

Stale Bread Pudding

Ingredients:

- 4-5 cups stale bread, torn or cubed (such as French bread, brioche, or challah)
- 2 cups milk (whole milk or any plant-based milk)
- 4 large eggs
- 1/2 cup granulated sugar
- 1 teaspoon vanilla extract
- 1/2 teaspoon ground cinnamon
- 1/4 teaspoon ground nutmeg
- Pinch of salt
- 1/2 cup raisins or other dried fruit (optional)
- Butter or cooking spray, for greasing the baking dish

Instructions:

Preheat the Oven:
- Preheat your oven to 350°F (175°C). Grease a baking dish (such as an 8x8-inch or 9x9-inch baking dish) with butter or cooking spray.

Prepare the Bread:
- Tear or cut the stale bread into bite-sized pieces and spread them evenly in the greased baking dish.

Prepare the Custard Mixture:
- In a mixing bowl, whisk together the eggs, sugar, vanilla extract, ground cinnamon, ground nutmeg, and salt until well combined.
- Gradually whisk in the milk until the mixture is smooth and uniform.

Combine Bread and Custard:
- Pour the custard mixture over the stale bread in the baking dish. Press down gently with a spoon or spatula to ensure all the bread pieces are soaked in the custard.
- If desired, sprinkle raisins or other dried fruit over the bread mixture.

Let it Sit:
- Allow the bread mixture to sit for about 15-20 minutes, pressing down occasionally with a spoon to help the bread absorb the custard.

Bake the Bread Pudding:
- Place the baking dish in the preheated oven and bake for 40-45 minutes, or until the bread pudding is set and golden brown on top.
- The pudding is done when a knife inserted into the center comes out clean.

Serve Warm:
- Remove the bread pudding from the oven and let it cool slightly.
- Serve warm, either on its own or with a scoop of vanilla ice cream, whipped cream, or a drizzle of caramel sauce.

Tips for Stale Bread Pudding:

- Use any type of stale bread you have on hand, such as French bread, brioche, challah, or even leftover dinner rolls.
- Customize the bread pudding by adding chopped nuts, chocolate chips, or different spices like cardamom or cloves.
- For a richer bread pudding, substitute some of the milk with heavy cream.
- Leftover bread pudding can be stored in the refrigerator for up to 3-4 days. Reheat individual portions in the microwave before serving.

Stale bread pudding is a delightful dessert that makes use of leftover bread and transforms it into a cozy and satisfying treat. Enjoy this classic recipe for a comforting dessert or sweet brunch dish!

Kale Stem Chips

Ingredients:

- Kale stems (from a bunch of kale)
- Olive oil or avocado oil
- Salt, to taste
- Optional seasonings: garlic powder, onion powder, paprika, cayenne pepper, or nutritional yeast

Instructions:

Preheat the Oven:
- Preheat your oven to 350°F (175°C).

Prepare the Kale Stems:
- Wash the kale stems thoroughly under cold water to remove any dirt or debris.
- Trim off the tough ends of the kale stems and discard.

Slice the Kale Stems:
- Using a sharp knife, slice the kale stems into thin, chip-like pieces. Aim for uniform thickness to ensure even baking.

Season the Kale Stems:
- Place the sliced kale stems in a bowl.
- Drizzle with olive oil or avocado oil, just enough to lightly coat the stems.
- Sprinkle with salt and any optional seasonings of your choice (garlic powder, onion powder, paprika, cayenne pepper, nutritional yeast, etc.). Toss to coat evenly.

Bake the Kale Stems:
- Arrange the seasoned kale stems in a single layer on a baking sheet lined with parchment paper or a silicone baking mat.
- Bake in the preheated oven for 12-15 minutes, or until the kale stems are crispy and golden brown around the edges. Keep an eye on them to prevent burning.

Cool and Enjoy:
- Remove the kale stem chips from the oven and let them cool on the baking sheet for a few minutes.
- Transfer the crispy kale stem chips to a serving bowl or plate.
- Enjoy them immediately as a crunchy snack or as a healthy topping for salads, soups, or grain bowls.

Tips for Making Kale Stem Chips:

- Ensure the kale stems are thoroughly dried after washing to help them crisp up in the oven.
- Experiment with different seasonings to create unique flavor combinations.
- Adjust the baking time based on the thickness of the kale stems and your desired level of crispiness.
- Store leftover kale stem chips in an airtight container at room temperature for up to 2-3 days. They may lose some crispiness over time, but you can re-crisp them in a low-temperature oven before serving.

Kale stem chips are a nutritious and delicious snack that's easy to make and perfect for using up kale stems that would otherwise be discarded. Enjoy these crunchy chips as a guilt-free treat!

Beet Stem Stir Fry

Ingredients:

- Beet stems (from a bunch of beets), washed and chopped
- 1 tablespoon olive oil or vegetable oil
- 2 cloves garlic, minced
- 1-inch piece of ginger, minced (optional)
- 1 small onion, sliced
- 1 bell pepper, sliced (any color)
- Soy sauce or tamari, to taste
- Sesame oil, for drizzling (optional)
- Salt and pepper, to taste
- Red pepper flakes, for heat (optional)
- Cooked rice or noodles, for serving

Instructions:

Prepare the Beet Stems:
- Wash the beet stems thoroughly under cold water. Trim off any tough ends and chop the stems into bite-sized pieces.

Heat the Oil:
- In a large skillet or wok, heat olive oil or vegetable oil over medium-high heat.

Sauté Aromatics:
- Add minced garlic and ginger (if using) to the hot oil. Sauté for about 30 seconds until fragrant.

Add Onion and Beet Stems:
- Add sliced onion and chopped beet stems to the skillet. Stir-fry for 3-4 minutes until the vegetables start to soften.

Incorporate Bell Pepper:
- Add sliced bell pepper to the skillet. Continue to stir-fry for another 2-3 minutes until all vegetables are tender-crisp.

Season the Stir Fry:
- Season the vegetables with soy sauce or tamari, to taste. Be cautious with the amount of soy sauce as it can be salty.
- Add salt, pepper, and red pepper flakes (if using) to adjust the seasoning.

Finish and Serve:
- Drizzle a little sesame oil over the stir fry for extra flavor (optional).
- Taste and adjust seasoning if needed.

- Remove the skillet from heat and serve the beet stem stir fry hot over cooked rice or noodles.

Tips for Making Beet Stem Stir Fry:

- Beet stems cook quickly, so make sure not to overcook them to retain their crunchiness.
- Feel free to add other vegetables like broccoli, snap peas, or mushrooms to the stir fry.
- Customize the seasoning with your favorite spices or sauces, such as hoisin sauce, sriracha, or oyster sauce.
- Garnish the beet stem stir fry with chopped green onions, cilantro, or toasted sesame seeds for extra freshness and texture.

Beet stem stir fry is a delicious and colorful dish that's packed with flavor and nutrients. Enjoy this simple and satisfying recipe as a side dish or light vegetarian meal!

Beef Stim Sir-Fry

Ingredients:

- Beet stems (from a bunch of beets), washed and chopped
- 1 tablespoon olive oil or vegetable oil
- 2 cloves garlic, minced
- 1-inch piece of ginger, minced (optional)
- 1 small onion, sliced
- 1 bell pepper, sliced (any color)
- Soy sauce or tamari, to taste
- Sesame oil, for drizzling (optional)
- Salt and pepper, to taste
- Red pepper flakes, for heat (optional)
- Cooked rice or noodles, for serving

Instructions:

Prepare the Beet Stems:
- Wash the beet stems thoroughly under cold water. Trim off any tough ends and chop the stems into bite-sized pieces.

Heat the Oil:
- In a large skillet or wok, heat olive oil or vegetable oil over medium-high heat.

Sauté Aromatics:
- Add minced garlic and ginger (if using) to the hot oil. Sauté for about 30 seconds until fragrant.

Add Onion and Beet Stems:
- Add sliced onion and chopped beet stems to the skillet. Stir-fry for 3-4 minutes until the vegetables start to soften.

Incorporate Bell Pepper:
- Add sliced bell pepper to the skillet. Continue to stir-fry for another 2-3 minutes until all vegetables are tender-crisp.

Season the Stir Fry:
- Season the vegetables with soy sauce or tamari, to taste. Be cautious with the amount of soy sauce as it can be salty.
- Add salt, pepper, and red pepper flakes (if using) to adjust the seasoning.

Finish and Serve:
- Drizzle a little sesame oil over the stir fry for extra flavor (optional).
- Taste and adjust seasoning if needed.

- Remove the skillet from heat and serve the beet stem stir fry hot over cooked rice or noodles.

Tips for Making Beet Stem Stir Fry:

- Beet stems cook quickly, so make sure not to overcook them to retain their crunchiness.
- Feel free to add other vegetables like broccoli, snap peas, or mushrooms to the stir fry.
- Customize the seasoning with your favorite spices or sauces, such as hoisin sauce, sriracha, or oyster sauce.
- Garnish the beet stem stir fry with chopped green onions, cilantro, or toasted sesame seeds for extra freshness and texture.

Beet stem stir fry is a delicious and colorful dish that's packed with flavor and nutrients.

Enjoy this simple and satisfying recipe as a side dish or light vegetarian meal!

Potato Peel Soup

Ingredients:

- Potato peels from about 4-5 medium potatoes
- 1 tablespoon olive oil or butter
- 1 onion, chopped
- 2 cloves garlic, minced
- 1 large carrot, diced
- 1 celery stalk, diced
- 4 cups vegetable or chicken broth
- 1 bay leaf
- 1 teaspoon dried thyme
- Salt and pepper, to taste
- 1/2 cup heavy cream or milk (optional, for creamier soup)
- Fresh parsley or chives, chopped (for garnish)

Instructions:

Prepare Potato Peels:
- Wash the potatoes thoroughly and peel them using a vegetable peeler, reserving the peels. You can leave a little bit of potato flesh on the peels for added flavor.

Cook the Aromatics:
- In a large pot or Dutch oven, heat olive oil or butter over medium heat. Add chopped onion, minced garlic, diced carrot, and diced celery. Sauté for 5-7 minutes until the vegetables start to soften.

Add Potato Peels:
- Add the potato peels to the pot and stir to combine with the sautéed vegetables.

Simmer with Broth and Seasonings:
- Pour in the vegetable or chicken broth, along with the bay leaf and dried thyme. Bring the mixture to a simmer.

Cook Until Potatoes are Tender:
- Cover the pot and simmer for about 20-25 minutes, or until the potato peels are tender and cooked through.

Blend the Soup:
- Remove the bay leaf from the soup.
- Use an immersion blender or transfer the soup to a blender in batches to purée until smooth and creamy.

Add Cream (Optional) and Adjust Seasoning:
- Stir in heavy cream or milk, if using, to make the soup creamier. Season with salt and pepper to taste.

Serve and Garnish:
- Ladle the potato peel soup into bowls. Garnish with chopped fresh parsley or chives.
- Serve hot and enjoy!

Tips for Potato Peel Soup:

- If you prefer a chunkier soup, you can blend only part of the soup and leave some potato peels intact.
- Customize the soup by adding other vegetables such as chopped spinach, kale, or peas.
- For extra flavor, you can stir in grated cheese (such as cheddar or Parmesan) at the end of cooking.
- Store leftover soup in an airtight container in the refrigerator for up to 3-4 days. Reheat gently on the stovetop or in the microwave before serving.

Potato peel soup is a simple and satisfying dish that's perfect for using up potato peels and creating a delicious meal. Enjoy this creamy and flavorful soup with crusty bread or a side salad for a comforting meal!

Avocado Seed Guacamole

Ingredients:

- 1 ripe avocado
- 1 avocado seed (washed and dried)
- 1 lime, juiced
- 1/4 cup finely chopped onion
- 1 small tomato, diced
- 1-2 tablespoons chopped cilantro
- Salt, to taste
- Optional: Jalapeño or serrano pepper, finely chopped (for heat)

Instructions:

Prepare the Avocado Seed:
- Wash the avocado seed thoroughly to remove any remaining avocado flesh.
- Use a knife to carefully slice the seed in half. Remove the inner seed from the outer skin (it will look like a large, smooth seed).

Grate the Avocado Seed:
- Use a microplane grater or a fine cheese grater to grate the avocado seed into a fine powder. You can also use a mortar and pestle to crush the seed into a powder.

Prepare the Guacamole:
- In a bowl, mash the ripe avocado with a fork until smooth.
- Add the grated avocado seed powder to the mashed avocado. The seed powder will add a nutty flavor and additional nutrients.
- Stir in the lime juice to prevent the avocado from browning and add a tangy flavor.

Add Remaining Ingredients:
- Mix in the finely chopped onion, diced tomato, chopped cilantro, and salt to taste.
- If you like spicy guacamole, add finely chopped jalapeño or serrano pepper for heat.

Adjust Seasoning:
- Taste the guacamole and adjust the seasoning as needed. Add more salt or lime juice according to your preference.

Serve and Enjoy:
- Transfer the avocado seed guacamole to a serving bowl.

- Serve with tortilla chips, vegetable sticks, or use as a topping for tacos, nachos, or sandwiches.

Tips for Avocado Seed Guacamole:

- The grated avocado seed adds a nutty and slightly bitter flavor to the guacamole. Start with a small amount and adjust to your taste preference.
- Use ripe avocados for the best texture and flavor in guacamole.
- Make the guacamole ahead of time and cover it tightly with plastic wrap (pressing the wrap directly onto the surface of the guacamole) to prevent browning.
- Experiment with additional ingredients such as garlic, cumin, or diced mango for a unique twist on traditional guacamole.

Avocado seed guacamole is a creative and flavorful way to make use of avocado seeds and create a delicious dip. Enjoy this unique guacamole with friends and family as a healthy snack or party appetizer!

Tomato Skin Salsa

Ingredients:

- Tomato skins from about 4-5 medium tomatoes
- 1 small onion, finely chopped
- 1-2 jalapeño peppers, seeded and finely chopped (adjust to taste)
- 2 cloves garlic, minced
- Juice of 1 lime
- 1/4 cup chopped fresh cilantro
- Salt and pepper, to taste

Instructions:

Prepare Tomato Skins:
- Collect tomato skins from peeled tomatoes. If you have whole tomatoes, blanch them in boiling water for a few seconds, then transfer to an ice water bath. The skins should easily peel off.

Chop Tomato Skins:
- Finely chop the tomato skins into small pieces. They will add texture and flavor to the salsa.

Combine Ingredients:
- In a bowl, combine the chopped tomato skins, finely chopped onion, jalapeño peppers, minced garlic, chopped cilantro, and lime juice.

Season and Mix:
- Season the salsa with salt and pepper, to taste. Adjust the amount of salt and lime juice based on your preference.

Chill (Optional):
- For best flavor, let the salsa chill in the refrigerator for at least 30 minutes to allow the flavors to meld together.

Serve and Enjoy:
- Stir the salsa before serving and adjust seasoning if needed.
- Serve the tomato skin salsa with tortilla chips, tacos, quesadillas, grilled meats, or use it as a topping for salads and bowls.

Tips for Tomato Skin Salsa:

- You can customize the salsa by adding additional ingredients such as diced bell peppers, corn, black beans, or mango for a unique twist.

- Adjust the level of spiciness by adding more or less jalapeño peppers, or leave the seeds in for extra heat.
- If you prefer a smoother texture, you can pulse the salsa in a food processor or blender for a few seconds.
- Store leftover salsa in an airtight container in the refrigerator for up to 3-4 days. The flavors will continue to develop over time.

Tomato skin salsa is a simple and delicious way to reduce food waste and create a flavorful condiment using tomato skins. Enjoy this homemade salsa as a versatile topping or dip for your favorite dishes!

Radish Top Pesto

Ingredients:

- Radish tops (greens) from a bunch of radishes, washed and roughly chopped
- 1/2 cup nuts or seeds (such as pine nuts, walnuts, almonds, or sunflower seeds)
- 2 cloves garlic, peeled
- 1/2 cup grated Parmesan cheese (or nutritional yeast for a vegan option)
- Juice of 1 lemon
- 1/2 cup extra-virgin olive oil
- Salt and pepper, to taste

Instructions:

Prepare Radish Tops:
- Wash the radish tops thoroughly under cold water to remove any dirt or debris. Pat dry with paper towels.

Toast Nuts or Seeds (Optional):
- If using nuts or seeds, toast them in a dry skillet over medium heat for a few minutes until lightly golden and fragrant. Let them cool before using.

Blend Ingredients:
- In a food processor or blender, combine the radish tops, toasted nuts or seeds, peeled garlic cloves, grated Parmesan cheese (or nutritional yeast), and lemon juice.
- Pulse several times to chop the ingredients.

Add Olive Oil:
- With the food processor or blender running, slowly drizzle in the extra-virgin olive oil until the pesto reaches your desired consistency. You may need to stop and scrape down the sides of the bowl with a spatula.

Season and Adjust:
- Season the radish top pesto with salt and pepper, to taste. Blend again to combine.

Taste and Adjust:
- Taste the pesto and adjust the flavors as needed. Add more lemon juice, salt, or Parmesan cheese according to your preference.

Serve and Enjoy:
- Transfer the radish top pesto to a bowl or jar.
- Use the pesto immediately as a sauce for pasta, spread for sandwiches or wraps, topping for roasted vegetables, or dip for bread and crackers.

Tips for Radish Top Pesto:

- Radish top pesto can be stored in an airtight container in the refrigerator for up to 5-7 days. For longer storage, you can freeze the pesto in ice cube trays and transfer the frozen cubes to a freezer bag for up to 3 months.
- Customize the pesto by experimenting with different nuts or seeds, such as pine nuts, walnuts, almonds, or sunflower seeds.
- For a dairy-free and vegan version, replace Parmesan cheese with nutritional yeast or skip the cheese altogether.
- Adjust the consistency of the pesto by adding more olive oil for a smoother texture or reducing the oil for a thicker pesto.

Radish top pesto is a versatile and flavorful sauce that transforms radish greens into a delicious culinary creation. Enjoy this vibrant pesto with various dishes and savor the fresh flavors of radish tops!

Citrus Peel Marmalade

Ingredients:

- 3-4 large citrus fruits (such as oranges, lemons, or grapefruits)
- 4 cups water
- 3 cups granulated sugar
- Optional: Additional flavorings like vanilla bean, cinnamon stick, or cloves

Instructions:

Prepare the Citrus Fruits:
- Wash the citrus fruits thoroughly under cold water to remove any dirt or wax. Use a vegetable peeler or sharp knife to carefully peel the outer zest from the fruits, avoiding the white pith as much as possible.

Slice and Remove Seeds:
- Slice the peeled citrus zest into thin strips or finely chop it, depending on your preference.
- Cut the peeled fruits in half and juice them to collect the juice. Reserve the seeds in a cheesecloth or muslin bag.

Cook the Citrus Peel:
- Place the chopped citrus zest strips or pieces in a large pot or saucepan. Add the water and the reserved citrus seeds (in a bag) to the pot.
- Bring the mixture to a boil over medium-high heat, then reduce the heat to low and simmer for about 30-40 minutes, until the peel is tender and softened.

Add Sugar and Flavorings:
- Remove the citrus seeds from the pot and discard them.
- Stir in the granulated sugar and any optional flavorings (such as a split vanilla bean, cinnamon stick, or cloves) into the pot with the softened citrus peel.

Simmer to Thicken:
- Bring the mixture back to a simmer over medium-low heat. Cook, stirring occasionally, for about 45-60 minutes, until the marmalade thickens and reaches a jam-like consistency. You can test the doneness by placing a small amount of the marmalade on a chilled plate; it should set and wrinkle when pushed with a finger.

Cool and Store:
- Once the marmalade reaches the desired consistency, remove the pot from heat and let it cool slightly.

- Transfer the citrus peel marmalade into clean, sterilized jars. Seal the jars tightly and allow them to cool completely at room temperature.
- Store the sealed jars of citrus peel marmalade in the refrigerator for up to several months. Once opened, consume within a few weeks.

Tips for Citrus Peel Marmalade:

- Use a combination of different citrus fruits for a more complex flavor profile.
- Adjust the amount of sugar according to your preference for sweetness.
- For a smoother marmalade, blend or pulse the cooked citrus peel mixture in a food processor or blender before adding the sugar.
- Experiment with different spices or herbs to customize the flavor of your citrus peel marmalade, such as cardamom, ginger, or rosemary.

Enjoy your homemade citrus peel marmalade spread on toast, stirred into yogurt, or used as a glaze for meats or desserts. This versatile preserve captures the bright essence of citrus fruits and makes a delightful addition to your pantry!

Apple Core Vinegar

Ingredients:

- Apple cores and peels (from 4-6 apples)
- 4 cups water (filtered or distilled)
- 1 tablespoon sugar (optional, to kickstart fermentation)
- Clean glass jar or container with a wide mouth
- Cheesecloth or coffee filter
- Rubber band or string
- Apple cider vinegar with mother (optional, as a starter)

Instructions:

Prepare the Apple Cores and Peels:
- Collect apple cores and peels from 4-6 apples. It's okay if they have some fruit flesh attached.

Place in a Glass Jar:
- Place the apple cores and peels into a clean glass jar or container with a wide mouth.

Make the Vinegar Solution:
- In a separate bowl, mix 4 cups of water with 1 tablespoon of sugar (if using). Stir until the sugar is dissolved.

Pour the Solution Over the Apple Scraps:
- Pour the water and sugar solution over the apple cores and peels in the glass jar, making sure they are fully submerged. Leave a little space at the top of the jar.

Cover and Secure:
- Cover the jar opening with a piece of cheesecloth or a coffee filter. Secure the cover with a rubber band or string to keep insects out while allowing air to flow.

Ferment the Vinegar:
- Place the jar in a warm, dark place (such as a kitchen cabinet or pantry) for about 2-3 weeks. Stir the contents gently every few days to aerate and promote fermentation.

Check for Fermentation:
- After a few weeks, you should start to see bubbles forming and notice a tangy smell, indicating that fermentation is occurring.

Strain and Transfer:

- Once the vinegar has reached your desired level of tanginess, strain out the apple cores and peels using a fine mesh sieve or cheesecloth. Discard the solids.

Optional Secondary Fermentation (with Mother):
- If you have apple cider vinegar with "mother" (the cloudy substance containing beneficial bacteria), you can add a splash to the strained apple vinegar to kickstart the development of the mother in your homemade vinegar.

Store the Apple Core Vinegar:
- Transfer the strained apple core vinegar to a clean glass bottle or jar with a tight-fitting lid. Store it in a cool, dark place like a pantry or cupboard.

Tips for Apple Core Vinegar:

- Use organic apples if possible, as they contain fewer pesticides and chemicals.
- Feel free to experiment with different types of apple varieties for unique flavors.
- You can use this homemade apple core vinegar in salad dressings, marinades, or as a natural household cleaner.
- Store the apple core vinegar in the refrigerator to prolong its shelf life and maintain freshness.

Homemade apple core vinegar is a sustainable and eco-friendly way to reduce food waste while creating a versatile and flavorful vinegar for culinary and household use. Enjoy the process of fermentation and the satisfaction of making your own vinegar from apple scraps!

Pineapple Core Smoothie

Ingredients:

- 1 cup pineapple core, chopped (from a fresh pineapple)
- 1 ripe banana, peeled and sliced
- 1 cup coconut water or water
- 1/2 cup plain Greek yogurt or coconut yogurt (optional, for creaminess)
- Juice of 1/2 lime or lemon (optional, for added tanginess)
- Honey or agave syrup, to taste (optional, for additional sweetness)
- Ice cubes (optional, for a chilled smoothie)

Instructions:

Prepare the Pineapple Core:
- Cut off the top and bottom of the pineapple. Stand the pineapple upright and carefully cut away the outer peel in strips, following the curve of the fruit.
- Cut the peeled pineapple into slices. Reserve the core for the smoothie.

Chop the Pineapple Core:
- Chop the pineapple core into small pieces that are easier to blend. The core is tough, so cutting it into smaller chunks will help in blending.

Combine Ingredients:
- In a blender, add the chopped pineapple core, sliced banana, coconut water or water, Greek yogurt or coconut yogurt (if using), and lime or lemon juice (if using).
- Optionally, add honey or agave syrup for additional sweetness, depending on your taste preference.

Blend Until Smooth:
- Blend all the ingredients together until smooth and creamy. If desired, add a few ice cubes to the blender to make a chilled smoothie.

Taste and Adjust:
- Taste the smoothie and adjust the sweetness or tartness by adding more honey, lime/lemon juice, or yogurt as needed.

Serve and Enjoy:
- Pour the pineapple core smoothie into glasses.
- Garnish with a pineapple wedge or mint leaves, if desired.
- Serve immediately and enjoy the tropical flavors!

Tips for Pineapple Core Smoothie:

- To make the smoothie vegan or dairy-free, use coconut yogurt or skip the yogurt altogether.
- Customize the smoothie by adding other fruits like mango, papaya, or strawberries.
- For a thicker smoothie, use frozen banana slices or add a handful of ice cubes.
- Pineapple core contains bromelain, an enzyme that may aid digestion. Enjoying the core in a smoothie is a tasty way to benefit from this enzyme.
- Use ripe pineapple for the best flavor and sweetness in the smoothie.

Enjoy this refreshing and nutritious pineapple core smoothie as a healthy breakfast, snack, or post-workout drink. It's a great way to use up the entire pineapple and reduce food waste while savoring tropical flavors!

Coffee Grounds Marinade

Ingredients:

- 1/4 cup used coffee grounds (cooled and dried)
- 1/4 cup olive oil or vegetable oil
- 2 tablespoons soy sauce or tamari (for gluten-free option)
- 2 tablespoons Worcestershire sauce
- 2 tablespoons balsamic vinegar or red wine vinegar
- 2 cloves garlic, minced
- 1 teaspoon Dijon mustard
- 1 teaspoon honey or maple syrup
- Salt and pepper, to taste

Instructions:

Prepare the Coffee Grounds:
- Collect 1/4 cup of used coffee grounds from freshly brewed coffee. Allow the coffee grounds to cool and dry out before using them in the marinade.

Mix the Marinade Ingredients:
- In a bowl, combine the cooled coffee grounds, olive oil or vegetable oil, soy sauce or tamari, Worcestershire sauce, balsamic vinegar or red wine vinegar, minced garlic, Dijon mustard, honey or maple syrup, salt, and pepper.

Whisk Until Well Combined:
- Whisk all the ingredients together until the marinade is well combined and emulsified. The coffee grounds will infuse the mixture with their flavor and texture.

Marinate the Meat:
- Place your choice of meat (such as steak, pork chops, or chicken breasts) in a shallow dish or resealable plastic bag.
- Pour the coffee grounds marinade over the meat, making sure it is fully coated. Use your hands to massage the marinade into the meat, ensuring even coverage.

Refrigerate and Marinate:
- Cover the marinated meat and refrigerate for at least 1-2 hours, or ideally overnight. The longer you marinate, the more the flavors will penetrate the meat.

Cook the Marinated Meat:
- Remove the meat from the marinade and discard any excess marinade.

- Cook the meat according to your preference, such as grilling, pan-searing, or baking. The coffee grounds will create a flavorful crust on the meat as it cooks.

Rest and Serve:
- Allow the cooked meat to rest for a few minutes before slicing or serving. This allows the juices to redistribute and the flavors to settle.

Enjoy Your Coffee Grounds-Marinated Meat:
- Serve the coffee-infused meat with your favorite side dishes, such as roasted vegetables, rice, or salad.

Tips for Coffee Grounds Marinade:

- Adjust the sweetness and acidity of the marinade by adding more or less honey/maple syrup and vinegar.
- For an extra kick of flavor, add a pinch of smoked paprika, chili powder, or cayenne pepper to the marinade.
- Use this marinade for different cuts of meat, seafood, or even tofu for a vegetarian option.
- If you prefer a smoother marinade texture, you can blend the ingredients in a food processor or blender before marinating the meat.

Enjoy the rich and robust flavors of coffee grounds-marinated meat for a delicious and memorable meal. This marinade is a great way to repurpose used coffee grounds and elevate your cooking with a unique twist!

www.ingramcontent.com/pod-product-compliance
Lightning Source LLC
LaVergne TN
LVHW061944070526
838199LV00060B/3965